ESCALATE

The Practical Guide to Get Yourself Unstuck and Build Lifelong Momentum

KYLE J. BROST, MBA

Stickhill Press

Denver, Colorado USA

https://kylebrost.com

Printed in the United States of America

Escalate: A Practical Guide to Getting Yourself Unstuck and Building Lifelong Momentum / Kyle Brost.

ISBN: 978-0-578-40727-2

Library of Congress Cataloging-in-Publication Data

Brost, Kyle J.

Escalate: the practical guide to get yourself unstuck and build lifelong momentum / Kyle

J. Brost, MBA

p cm.

1. Self-help techniques. 2. Business

2018912665

When it is obvious

that the goals cannot be reached,

don't adjust the goals, adjust the

action steps.

- Confucius

escalate

[es-kuh-leyt]

1. To increase in intensity, magnitude, etc.
2. become or cause to become more intense or serious
3. Increase rapidly
4. to increase in extent, volume, number, amount, intensity, or scope

LEARN MORE

Use this code ESCALATE15893 to get 35% off the Escalate Course.

Visit: kylebrost.com/escalate

Access the most powerful resource to get yourself unstuck and achieve your biggest goal yet.

You'll get access to...

- **The comprehensive Escalate Assessment with a personalized jumpstart guide**
- **15+ Video modules**
- **Exclusive tools, templates, and guides to ensure your progress**
- **The complete outsourcing guide and checklist**
- **Weekly Live Q&A webinars and all recorded webinars**
- **FAQs and support from others just like you**

For free supplemental resources on Escalate, please visit:

https://kylebrost.com/escalate

Table of Contents

PREFACE

The book *Escalate* started as a challenge to myself, but the challenge wasn't to write a book. It was to produce something accessible and meaningful to everyone. A lofty challenge no doubt. I wanted to take something complicated and simplify it. As Albert Einstein is quoted as saying, "The definition of genius is taking the complex and making it simple."

That's not to say that what I've done is genius. It's that my work in strategy and impact has taken me to the edges of theory and the abstract. However, when it comes to results, theories and abstract concepts can only take you so far.

While I love pondering things deeply and exploring the theoretical, I have witnessed firsthand how difficult it can be to translate theory into meaningful action. I needed a topic to cover and considering the intent of simplifying something complex into something actionable; I wondered, why not start with that—taking action? And so I did, I wrote this simple book on how to take action.

I chose to call the book *Escalate* because the term perfectly summarizes the key concept taught here, which is that when your effort falls short, you must increase it rapidly in "intensity and magnitude."

This book will not be for everyone, it may be too simple in its recommendations, too intuitive to those who are masters of taking action. However, that is the purpose, to layout as simply as possible the principles that encourage and enable you to take meaningful action.

To succeed at this, I focused on turning even those principles into practical advice. In speaking with many of you about where you struggle to take action, I heard time and time again, "If you want to make it simple, stop telling me the principles and give me the step-by-step process." Thus, in the following pages, I present to you the principles of taking action and the step-by-step process of *Escalate*.

It will be up to you, the reader, to determine if I've done so successfully.

DEDICATION

This has been an incredible journey, one that I could not have done alone. I don't say that lightly. I literally could not have accomplished what I have without the support of innumerable individuals.

I'm so grateful to my wife and children for the sacrifices they've made to support me in this work.

To the many mentors, influencers, associates, critics, reviewers, and friends—all I can say is thank you from the bottom of my heart. This is not my product alone, it is a team made product, and for this I am both humbled and grateful.

Introduction

When you hear the word *escalate*, you might think of conflict. In fact, as I shared the draft of this book with colleagues, one of the most frequent questions asked was, "Why are you using a word with so much negative association for the title?"

The answer is that at its very core, this book is about conflict. The internal conflict you experience every day in turning your thoughts and intentions into meaningful actions. And just as other conflicts often escalate before resolution, you want to escalate this internal conflict of yours.

Remember, *escalate* is to "increase rapidly in intensity or magnitude." When your internal conflict has you stuck, that's exactly what you must do—you must increase your efforts rapidly in intensity, volume, and magnitude.

Some people out there are intimidated by the idea of increasing their effort. They think, "I'm already giving everything I've got"! You, however, will come to understand through this book, how simple and doable escalating your efforts is. You will come to thrive on personal escalations, achieving more than you ever have, with less time and in fact, less energy.

I will forewarn you, this book is repetitive. You will see the word *escalate* hundreds of times. This is not an accident, it is intentional. When your progress slows, you take missteps, or experience failure, you should immediately *escalate.*

There should be no pause for consideration, no moment of confusion because *escalate* has been ingrained into your very nature through repetition. You are the only one who has the power to *escalate,* but you do have the power. *Escalate* will become your most potent tool to live up to your potential because it is your potential and it is real.

Through all my years of running my own businesses, working with organizations and leaders (including numerous Fortune 500 companies), and training over 1500+ leaders, I have noticed a few recurring elements that stand out above the rest.

A few years ago, I started to synthesize these fundamentals of action and achievement. One of the end results was the genesis of *Escalate*, the culmination of which is this book that you are reading now. These principles will help you go from beginning to end on each of your goals.

Along this journey to developing *Escalate*, I discovered *The Art of Strategic Reaction* through continued work with clients. *The Art of Strategic Reaction* is a set of strategic thinking and emotional agility tools that teach you how to react to uncertainty and emotion in strategic ways, making use of your full potential. The principles of *Escalate* and *The Art of Strategic Reaction* build upon each other—you may use the power of *Escalate* without *The Art of Strategic Reaction*, and vice versa.

However, when used together, these two practices act as propellants, getting you to where you need to be much smoother and faster.

You can learn more about *The Art of Strategic Reaction* at kylebrost.com/asr.

In 2006, I started a business-to-business outside sales company, selling discounted freight and air freight services in Kansas City, KS. Although I had run a small business before, at 24 years old, I was not an experienced nor expert entrepreneur. So why did I leap?

For six months prior to starting my business, I worked as a sales rep. Within the first two months, I was leading the country in sales, enlisted more clients and revenue dollars than other reps. From the start, I knew one thing: if I wasn't getting the sales, I needed to work harder until I did. This was a successful approach that I carried into my own business.

However, over the years, I began to see flaws. Although I could achieve more success by working harder, I continued to rely on the same limited set of methods. When sales slowed, I merely knocked more doors. Eventually, the results dwindled. Inevitably I would run into the same folks over and over again. I had learned how to work harder, but I had not discovered how to work smarter and it was killing my business.

Several years later, while working as a consultant, I noticed something startling with my clients. We would start our engagements with lofty goals and tasks for everyone, so that we could achieve them. Yet when the work began, my clients would often fail to accomplish the assigned tasks.

As uncompleted tasks piled up, one of two things would happen, either they would try to change the goal, or they would choose smaller efforts to complete it. These smaller efforts always had the same effect: progress would stall, and energy would be lost.

My clients would lose momentum and eventually get stuck.

The underlying assumption was that if they couldn't carry out the effort they had originally planned, maybe they could accomplish smaller tasks that required less effort. This was rarely the case.

Instead, it resulted in missed goals. What they did not realize was that they weren't choosing smaller tasks, they were choosing weaker methods. And these weaker methods would never have the power to propel them forward.

And so, for all their good intentions and desires to move forward, they still found themselves stuck.

Here is an example to illustrate the risk of choosing weaker methods, or as I call it, de-escalating.

Much of my childhood was spent on a family farm in Wyoming. An all too frequent scenario was that of getting a farm truck stuck in the mud. When this happens, you use whatever methods are available to get unstuck.

Often the first mistake made in this scenario is to try and power the truck out by accelerating. You try to get unstuck by doing more of the very thing that got you stuck. You apply the principle of insanity, trying the same thing repeatedly, expecting a different result.

When that doesn't work, according to the belief that you should de-escalate to get unstuck, you try to push the vehicle out. When that doesn't work, you tell yourself, "This is too big an effort, the truck is too heavy for me to move, I should try something that's not as difficult." So, you grab a shovel and start digging.

Soon you realize that this method won't work either. Again, you tell yourself, "This too is too much, a shovel full of mud is too heavy and is wearing me out, I should try something that's not as difficult." So, you start digging with your hands. Now, this is doable, you can get yourself to dig with your hands because it's simple and easy. However, after two hours of digging, you're not any closer to getting unstuck than when you started.

Here you are two hours into the scenario, and you've managed to get yourself more stuck by working harder. Not to mention you've exhausted yourself because of these weak methods.

This is the precise scenario you put yourself into when you only know how to work harder but not smarter. You choose weaker and weaker methods to accomplish your goals. When pushing doesn't work, you don't need a weaker method of getting unstuck, you need a more powerful one. Instead of de-escalating to your hands, you need to *Escalate*. Try having three or four people push, and if that doesn't work, go get a tractor to pull yourself out.

Now, you may see the absurdity of trying to dig a farm truck out of the mud with your hands. That's the point. You may never try to do this. Yet, how often do you do it in your personal life? How often do you resort to doing the minimum on something important?

The *Escalate Process* came out of similar experiences with my clients. To address the problems that arise from working harder or choosing weaker methods, I designed a prescriptive approach that can be followed as a process to achieve your goals. Drawing on my own experiences and research on desire, action, and momentum, it is a method that has proven time and again to get people unstuck and build momentum.

While I initially developed *Escalate* to help my business and clients, others including friends, family, and associates have used it to reach personal goals such as completing a 70.3 Half-Ironman triathlon and launching a home business. I too have noticed that my own successes, both in work and in life, have come about through the application of these principles, the *Escalate Process* I offer here.

Escalate is now offered as a full online course! The comprehensive course includes exclusive videos, templates, podcasts, and practices not contained in the book. You can access the course today at kylebrost.com/escalate.

Let's dive in!

Section Outlines

Section 1: Breaking Down Motivation

Motivation is one of the most misunderstood and elusive concepts in human performance. Unfortunately, too many confuse excitement and enthusiasm for motivation. This confusion leads to unproductive excitement and wasted energy. People run around energized and excited, but in circles, not moving toward their goals.

- **Action + Desire = Progress**. Don't confuse excitement for motivation, the only way to know if someone is motivated is if they take action. If you're reading books, listening to podcasts, creating plans, those all indicate you have desire. All you need is action. While doing things such as reading, listening, and planning may be considered forms of taking action, *Escalate* is focused on taking measured action that directly moves you toward your goal. While progress is not dependent on desire, there are three factors that produce desire. They include alternatives, methods, and beliefs.
    - *Alternatives*. Alternatives are the first factor that produces desire. It is the recognition of alternatives to the current results you're getting. These can come from extreme pain or from seeing a higher level of results to aspire to. Ultimately, they are simply different results or experiences than what you have—alternatives produce a perceived need.

- *Methods*. Methods are things you believe produce your desired alternatives. They include resources, actions, circumstances, and connections. The key is your confidence that these things can produce the results or experiences you want. You must believe the methods will produce your desired alternative or they will be ineffective at building desire.
- *Beliefs*. The last factor to desire is a belief in yourself. It is one thing to believe certain actions or resources (methods) can produce the results you want. It is another to believe that you can produce the results you want. Belief is confidence that you can carry out the methods and thereby achieve your desired alternative.

While desire is a factor in achieving your goals, it is not the primary factor, nor is it even necessary to get started. For the most important factor to successful achievement, we explore Action in Section Two: The Action Principles.

Section 2: The Action Principles

The second section teaches core insights of action and momentum, in other words, what we know about action and momentum through research, case studies, anecdotes, and personal experience.

We start with the principles of action because they have broad application. By learning and applying the principles, you will be able to understand why the *Escalate Process* is built the way it is and how it is so effective.

These insights aren't intended to lecture you about what you should do; they are intended to help you understand action and momentum, to inspire you to spot opportunities and to create your plan. We will examine how:

A. Action perpetuates action. Taking any meaningful action will inspire more significant action, no matter how small it is. So, you should worry more about simply taking action than about which action you take.

B. Progress is powerful. Seeing progress is the single most motivating force, so learn to recognize progress in all its forms and learn to make it visible.

C. Extraordinary is the result of ordinary actions. Extraordinary is the result of countless tiny ordinary actions that accumulate to produce something extraordinary.

D. Failure is evidence of your greater potential. Don't be discouraged by your failures, recognize them as evidence that you have greater things yet to be achieved, and that's exciting!

E. Building momentum is easier than starting over. Getting started can take seven times more energy than building momentum when you are already going.

F. Unintentional habits are massive lost opportunities. When you follow routine too much, you go on autopilot and miss opportunities to be productive. The good news is that you can break the cycle and build new habits.

G. Goal-oriented action chains are productivity powerhouses. It has been said that flexibility is the key to power, but preparation is the key to flexibility. Productivity chains are all about preparation.

H. You'll do what's easy to do. You can put all the barriers in place to avoid doing the wrong things, but does that actually make the right things easier to do?

I. Paring down decisions frees up energy. Humans make thousands of decisions every day, if you can eliminate a few of those, you free up bandwidth.

J. Emotional goals are powerful goals. For anything to sustain, there must be a "why." Keep your purpose front and center to give you energy and ensure sustainability.

Section 3: The Process

The third section of this book contains the *Escalate Process.* This process pulls the principles of action and momentum into a clearly defined step-by-step process. The *Escalate Process* leverages insights about action and momentum, and the three core principles of getting things done. It is a prescriptive method, an overview of which can be viewed in the *Escalate Process* Map at the beginning of Section 3. Its primary focus is on getting unstuck and building momentum as you navigate your goals. While you could use it for common everyday goals, its real power is in getting you unstuck and building momentum toward the big goals that you are struggling to complete. You'll also find some rethinking of general perceptions here. They include:

A. Start Small. Most literature and programs will tell you that you need to take "massive action" to accomplish goals. They will ask you to start huge! That is false. We know that extraordinary achievements are not an action, they are a result, the culmination of small, simple steps that accumulate over time. When you start big, there is a real risk you will quickly feel uninspired when an inevitable hurdle comes your way. Deciding to de-escalate your efforts, taking smaller and smaller efforts in the hope of making progress will not compel you.

So instead of doing it this way, you need to break your big goal into manageable tasks and start small with a realistic goal. By taking this approach, you can always build up to something bigger (i.e., *Escalate*). It's much easier and better for morale to *Escalate* than it is to scale down your efforts.

This principle is contrary to the popular idea that de-escalating and picking a task that you see as "more achievable," will help you move forward. All that does is encourage you to take weaker and weaker steps toward achieving your goal. With each reduced effort, or selection of lesser actions, your ability to achieve your goal becomes less and less. Instead, begin small and methodically increase the power of your efforts by escalating.

Whenever you fail at one method of achieving something, you should choose a more powerful way, not a weaker one. For example, if working on a goal for 10 minutes a day hasn't gotten you to where you need to be, confide in a buddy and plan to do it for 30 minutes a day instead. By starting small, this will enable you to escalate and select increasingly powerful methods of accomplishing your goals without losing your progress.

B. Escalate: Whenever your method of accomplishing a task fails, you want to escalate your method. You will want choose a MORE powerful way of getting it done, not a LESS powerful way. Remember, it does not make any sense to choose an inferior route. If the course you just tried failed, you must select a more powerful one.

Don't fall into the infamous pattern of insanity by repeating the same thing over and over again but expecting a different result.

C. Prune: Sometimes projects get stuck because you have thrown too many ideas and methods into the mix. Planning and streamlining the tasks ahead is essential. You have to be decisive about what you will AND won't do. Pruning is the effort of consciously and intentionally choosing what you WON'T do. By pruning some activities, you free up attention, energy, and resources to focus on the most important things.

Don't just accept tradeoffs, be intentional, choose your actions, and follow-through.

Section 4: The Practice

The fourth and concluding section of this book puts the *Escalate* Process into practice. It is a set of simple tools and examples to strengthen your use of the principles and process of *Escalate*. The tools and examples are supplemented by the *Escalate* Facebook Group, which is a closed group for those committed to sharing their experiences. The comprehensive list of tools and resources can be accessed through the *Escalate* online course. These tools and resources include:

A. The Escalate Playbook. A quick reference decision chart to layout the full process and keep you on track.

B. Top ActionHacks. This is the Bonus: 23 Proven Hacks to Beat Procrastination. They are the 23 most simple and practical ways to get yourself to take action.

Join the Escalate Facebook Group Here or Access the Full Escalate Course Here (kylebrost.com/escalate).

SECTION 1: MOTIVATION IS A LIE!

CHAPTER 1

Motivation is a Lie!

"Desire is the absurdity that holds open the infinity of possibility"

– WENDY FARLEY

You've been lied to. Your entire life, you've been taught that you must be motivated, or you will fail. You've been fed the books, the lessons, and the speeches all designed to increase your motivation.

The problem is that everything you've been taught about motivation is a lie. Motivation is not the thing you believe it is.

Common beliefs confuse excitement for motivation. If you're not excited, you're not motivated. And without this excitement, you'll fail. I have sad news; this confused motivation is not the fountain of lifelong productivity you've been searching for.

Let's see if I'm right about this.

You've been taught that motivation is some mysterious mix of emotion and energy that when built up high enough initiates super-human work ethic. Those who aren't super-human or productive simply lack motivation.

It's been presented to you like the superpower meter in a video game. That when you have the right mindset and work on it long enough, you will reach capacity, unleashing your superhuman self and unlimited potential.

So, here you are, diligently working to fill your motivation meter until someday your excitement reaches the tipping point. You no longer struggle with procrastination and now have the indispensable energy to accomplish everything you've ever dreamed of.

If you're not out crushing it, hustling 24/7, grinding your side hustle, or just plain excited about life, your motivation meter just hasn't reached this magic tipping point. So, you go on trying to fill it, waiting for that moment when something clicks, you're suddenly excited about life and are so driven you no longer need sleep.

Sound about right?

It's easy to see how you've learned this. One online dictionary defines motivation as "the level of desire you have for doing something," another as "something which incites activity," and yet another as "enthusiasm for doing something."

In the thesaurus, synonyms for motivation include desire, encouragement, interest, and excitement.

THAT SAID, THE BIGGEST LIE ISN'T THAT MOTIVATION IS EXCITEMENT. THE BIGGEST LIE IS THAT YOU NEED MOTIVATION TO ACHIEVE YOUR GOALS.

How do we know this is a lie? It's simple, there are billions of people excitedly running around while not actually accomplishing anything. How many people have you met who are always busy, always running around and yet not making any progress?

If motivation is what you've been taught, this excitement would translate to results. I'm sorry to tell you but it doesn't. Most of those excited folks are just wasting time, wearing themselves out not achieving their goals.

On the other hand, you accomplish things every day that you're not excited about. You're not excited to pick up dog poop from your yard, yet you do it. You dread that chunky green smoothie every morning, yet you drink it.

So, if confused excitement doesn't produce results, and you accomplish things every day that you're not excited about, what is the truth about motivation?

The truth is that you don't need motivation to accomplish your goals.

Motivation is not the path to your success and is not equal to progress. When you understand this, you realize you can move toward your goals today, without motivation!

Instead, action and desire are the keys to progress. With this understanding, you have learned the progress equation.

ACTION *+ DESIRE = PROGRESS*

This equation trumps excitement and so-called motivation every day of the week.

The one surefire way to know if someone is progressing is if they take action. It's the only way to know. Action is inseparable from progress. Anyone can tell you they are motivated, but will you believe them if they haven't left the couch in three weeks?

For this reason, the bulk of this book will cover the principles of action and which actions to take. However, so there's no confusion, you'll want to learn a few principles of desire first. The most beautiful thing is that you can start and make progress on your goals without desire! And, I'll show you how.

This is why action always precedes desire in the progress equation, because action is the building block of all desire, progress, and achievement. It is the starting and the ending point. It's important to always write the progress equation leading with action, as a reminder to yourself that you don't need desire to start or make progress on your goals.

However, so there's no confusion, you'll want to learn a few things about desire, so that when the time comes, you can leverage it to amplify your results. While it is not the most important factor to progress, leveraging it can magnify and sustain your progress. You don't need desire to start, but it will help you keep going.

There are three factors that produce desire. They are alternatives, methods, and beliefs. All three of these factors can be deliberately developed.

Alternatives

The first place that desire comes from is alternatives. This happens when you are exposed to alternative results than the ones you're getting. It could be that you're in a place of pain and you see an alternative without that pain.

For example, you've lost your job and are struggling to put food on the table, but you see an alternative where food is abundant, and finances aren't a constant worry.

It could also be that you're comfortable but see a higher place of attainment. While your day-to-day life may not be painful, the recognition that your life could be better will create discomfort.

Either way, recognizing an alternative to your current state is where desire starts. If you are never in a place to see these alternatives, you never build the desire to reach them. The key is contrast between where you are today and where you could be.

A lack of alternatives most often surfaces as complacency. Because you cannot imagine an alternative reality, you become complacent with your current reality. When you see an alternative reality as possible, it's hard to be content with your current one.

These alternatives can be simple yet profound in nature as in the real example of Shin Dong-hyuk in the book *Escape from Camp 14: One Man's Remarkable Odyssey from North Korea to Freedom in the West.*[1]

Shin Dong-hyuk was born into Camp 14, a political prison in North Korea. His entire life was controlled within the walls of the prison. He had no education and no insight into alternatives; he was never exposed to an alternative way of living or being, so he had nothing to desire.

Except food.

Within the camp, food rations were meek, so food became the one thing Shin Dong-hyuk desired more than anything else. He simply desired more of it, going to great lengths to obtain just a few extra grains of rice.

If his desire to get a few extra grains of rice was strong, imagine how strong it was when Shin learned about hamburgers from another prisoner.

With the knowledge of a food with different textures, flavors, and scents, Shin now had an alternative. Not only was there an alternative where food was abundant, but there was an alternative where it had variety.

This simple contrast created enough desire for Shin to eventually escape from Camp 14 and make it to South Korea. He was the first person born into a North Korean prison to ever escape to the West.

You can discover alternatives and build desire by surrounding yourself with a diverse group of people. Most people spend their time around others most like them, and this tendency restricts access to alternatives.

By surrounding yourself with others from diverse backgrounds, you expose yourself to alternatives.

Additionally, you can try new things and visit new places. Anything you do to expose yourself to different people, places, and experiences will reveal alternatives. With exposure to enough alternatives, some of them will create a contrast so great that you cannot ignore it.

No matter where you are in life or how much you've achieved, I promise you, there is an even greater alternative for you out there. You, and only you can discover what it is but when you do, it will drive you to make progress daily.

What is the one element of your life that you long to change? What is the alternative you can see that makes you uncomfortable with where you are today?

When you see alternatives to the life you're living, you build desire. However, that desire will be amplified when you learn the methods for reaching that alternative.

Methods

Alternatives are a great start to build desire. However, alternatives are more powerful when you see a way to reach them. The second factor to desire is methods.

Methods are the ways in which an alternative can become your reality. If you cannot see ways to attain an alternative, the alternative will struggle to build desire.

A lack of methods often surfaces as criticism and pessimism. You may learn a path to a new way of living, but rather than finding hope in it, you find only flaws and criticize it. When this is the case, explore why you are choosing to criticize. This type of criticism is a choice. You will also want to explore more than one path to reach your desired alternative.

Shin Dong-hyuk could have been exposed to an alternative where food was abundant and diverse, but if he had no understanding of how to make it a reality, then his desire would have faded. During his time in Camp 14, Shin witnessed many attempts to escape, some of them successful.

Because of this, Shin Dong-hyuk knew there were methods to reach his desired alternative. He was able to map out a potential path.

The key to methods is that you believe they will produce the alternative. This is where some fall short, they hear from others the steps to achieve an alternative, but they do not believe those steps will be effective for them personally.

They criticize and doubt by saying things like, "That won't work for me because..." rather than choosing to see how it can work for them.

In addition to doubting the methods, you can also see too many of them. When this happens, it can be difficult to choose a course of action, which will damper your desire. As we will talk about later in the book, this is called paralysis by analysis.

You want to use methods to build your desire. They will help you map out potential paths to your desired alternative making it even more compelling. Talk to others who have done it, be realistic about yourself, and map out a potential path to success. By seeing a path to your desired alternative, it will build your desire to pursue it. You will learn how to identify methods in Section Three: The Escalate Process.

While seeing a clear path toward your desired alternative will build desire, there is one factor that can overcome doubts about the path.

The more you believe that the methods will produce the desired alternative, the greater your desire to pursue it. However, it is one thing to believe that a specific method will produce the desired alternative, it is another to believe that you can carry out those methods and attain the desired result for yourself.

Beliefs

It is possible to see an alternative reality and to believe there is a way to attain it, but not believe in yourself. In this scenario, you doubt your personal ability to carry out the methods and achieve the alternative. Therefore, belief is the third factor to desire.

A lack of belief most often surfaces as fear or doubt. You may truly desire a different reality and believe there is a path to reach it. However, you may at the same time doubt your own ability to carry it out. You might also fear trying your hardest and still failing.

You don't have to believe you can chart the course to an alternative perfectly, you only need to believe that you can learn from failure and adapt as necessary.

Belief in self is powerful and can overcome deficiencies in methods. When belief in yourself is strong enough, you can move forward even when the path forward is uncertain. This is because while you understand that the path may not be the perfect one, you are certain that you can adapt and adjust.

If you have an alternative that you desire and know the methods to attain it, but don't believe that you yourself can carry out those methods and produce that alternative, your desire will die. You must believe that you, as an individual, have the power to carry out the methods and obtain the desired alternative.

Following the Escalate Process itself will build your belief, because you will make progress and achieve your goals. You can also build belief in yourself by engaging two practices right now. They are gratitude and solutions.

Whenever you sense that self-doubt is creeping in, immediately do two things. First, write a detailed list of five things you are grateful for. Doubt triggers a chain reaction that can quickly spiral out of control and lead to stress and anxiety and causes you to give up on your ideas as a coping mechanism. By forcing yourself to shift the thought process away from doubt to gratitude, you trigger a reaction that produces optimism.

Once you've completed your gratitude list, your brain is now primed for solutions. Solutions are an optimistic approach to problems and you've triggered optimism through your gratitude list. Your solutions will be more powerful and your belief in them stronger. When this approach becomes habit, you will create solutions to the biggest of challenges.

You are capable—don't let doubt ever cause you to deny that.

A Note About Desire and Mental Health

While the sum of this book is focused on how to identify which actions to take and get yourself to take them, I also understand that some reading this are in a different place, lacking even the desire to aspire.

This is a challenging place to be, and it's important to acknowledge that there are many reasons for that—some of them relating to mental health, for which this book is not a suitable resource.

If you are experiencing an overwhelming lack of desire, meaning that you have no desire to do anything, even those things that you typically find enjoyable, please consult with a mental health professional

One resource is the Substance Abuse and Mental Health Services Administration National Hotline 1-800-662-HELP (4357)

Quick Tips to Increase Your Desire:

- *Start where you are, even if that is with only hope. There are times that you may not have the desire and that's okay! Do you at least hope or want to have the desire? If so, start there. Begin by allowing yourself to daydream. Fantasize about a goal and what it would feel like if you were to accomplish it. Then, shift your daydreaming to seeking out alternatives.*
- *Earnestly strive to learn. A willingness to learn is the seed of desire. If you will plant it and spend time*

nurturing it daily, it will grow. Eventually, that growth will have no other place to go than to action. This is NOT about building excitement so you can be energized without direction. The best form of learning is through exposure to different people, places, and experiences. Start with something you wouldn't typically learn from or about.

- *Identify and write down all of the ways in which you already have desire. These might include an interest in learning, willingness to brainstorm plans, and even a simple sense of hope. By acknowledging that you already have desire, you'll be forced to direct your attention to actions. The stronger the evidence of your desire, the more crucial it is to take action now.*

- *Test taking action. You do not need strong desire in order to test action. There are dozens of things you hate and do not want to do, yet somehow find a way to do them. When you find yourself stuck and lacking desire, test small actions.*

- *Be brutally honest with yourself. There is a difference between admiring what another has achieved and being driven to achieve the same thing. When you pursue something because you think you should, rather than because you truly want to, you will get stuck. Focus on your uniqueness and strengths and be brutally honest about what you're interested in.*

Action, the Other Half of the Equation

In the same way you learned that excitement equals motivation, you also learned that it precedes action. This is the primary reason you've been trying to fill your motivation meter. The most reassuring information I can give you is that excitement, motivation, and desire do not have to precede action.

While desire is part of the progress equation, there is no mysterious and arbitrary meter of desire that must be filled in order to take action. Action can and should precede desire and then the two can reinforce one another.

This is why the progress equation is always written as, Action + Desire = Progress.

The more action you take, the greater the desire you'll build. The greater the desire you build, the easier it will be to sustain those actions. This reinforcing process is so powerful that if you enlist even a fraction of it, you'll accomplish far more than you yet imagine.

Desire magnifies your action, but before you start, to act is the only choice you have. You will want to acknowledge that before we can go any further together.

You see, your life is comprised of three things, and only three things. What you think, what you feel, and what you do. But only one of these has the power to influence the world around you. What you do. Action.

I learned this in a humorous way as a child. While working with my grandfather on our family farm, I would often complain about the tasks we needed to perform. In the dry climate of Wyoming, we used flood irrigation to water our crops.

This work was physical and dirty, requiring us to move hundreds of small metal siphon tubes. One day while complaining to my grandfather I said, "I wish I didn't have to do this!" To which he replied, "Well, wish in one hand and crap in the other and tell me which one fills up first."

While there is a crapload of humor in this story, his point was clear. Wishing alone would leave me empty-handed. Action was the only choice.

Progress, the Product of the Equation

Now, if you're like me and enjoy digging into the equation, trying to find flaws in it, then you may have questioned the last part of the equation, progress. I mean, this book guarantees that it will help you achieve your goals! Why not replace progress with results or success?

To answer that, let's dive into a hypothetical.

Let's assume you're trying to reach a goal. You want to build a business. You want to invent a product, solve a problem, get fit, or strengthen a relationship. You have two choices.

1. The first choice is to do nothing. With this choice, you will gain nothing and lose nothing. You'll be empty handed, guaranteed.

2. The second choice is to take action.

The answer is simple. Of course, you'd take action!

But what if the chances of achieving your desired result are one in one hundred? That means that in one hundred attempts, you will fail ninety-nine times and achieve your desired result only once.

Which do you choose?

While failing to achieve your desired result ninety-nine times out of a hundred is hypothetical, the question is not. You choose between these two options daily. So, what if you fail dozens of times, is there no value in failure?

Progress is what you care about, and progress comes from action, regardless of the results. You learn from failure. If you fail ninety-nine times, you will experience what doesn't work ninety-nine times over, and you will progress.

In the process, you will grow to understand what works, along with insights and principles that can be applied to future situations. Failure on your way to achieving a goal won't just help you achieve that goal, it will prepare you to achieve bigger goals.

Consider Thomas Edison, who while working tirelessly to improve his storage battery, tried several thousand chemical combinations. In Frank Dyer and T. C. Martin's authorized biography *Edison: His Life and Inventions,* Edison's friend and associate Walter S. Mallory said the following about these experiments:[2]

"This [the research] had been going on more than five months, seven days a week when I was called down to the laboratory to see him [Edison]. I found him at a bench about three feet wide and twelve feet long, on which there were hundreds of little test cells that had been made up by his corps of chemists and experimenters. I then learned that he had thus made over nine thousand experiments in trying to devise this new type of storage battery but had not produced a single thing that promised to solve the question. Given this immense amount of thought and labor, my sympathy got the better of my judgment, and I said: 'Isn't it a shame that with the tremendous amount of work you have done you haven't been able to get any results?'

"Edison turned on me like a flash, and with a smile replied: 'Results! Why, man, I have gotten lots of results! I know several thousand things that won't work!'"

This story illustrates a key insight. Whether your results are successful or unsuccessful does not dictate progress. Progress happens when you take action and sustain it via desire along the way.

Fortunately for us, Edison understood this principle. If he had not, many generations could have missed out on interior lighting and films.

Isolated actions don't have the power to achieve the extraordinary, but your ability to learn from your mistakes and improve your approach—your ability to iterate—is where the power of action is found. And each action, each iteration is progress.

Want help working through setbacks and adversity on the way to your goal? Join the Escalate Facebook group at https://www.facebook.com/groups/escalateprocess/

You want to start with the one principle that underlies every important accomplishment in human history: ACTION. Tear down what you've learned about motivation. Success does not start with motivation, it starts with action. You'll love the freedom and control of your results you gain through this understanding.

The irony in all of this is that while the world is waiting to build up their motivation meter before they take action, the fastest way to build desire...is to take action. Five minutes of action toward a goal will build more desire than five hours trying to fill your motivation meter.

Need proof that you don't have to start with desire? Just look at how much is invested in free samples annually. Why? Because marketers know that if they can get you to take a small action first, your desire will grow, and so too will your action.

How many times have you tried a sample at a big-box membership club, only to find yourself walking out with enough gouda infused chimichangas to host the annual block party?

Remember that while Action + Desire = Progress, action is all you need to get started.

Don't spend another minute trying to fill your fictional motivation meter! Instead take action, any action no matter how small. Just. Take. Action. If you fail 9,000 times like Edison, you will still be moving forward.

Tomorrow billions of people will go on with their days and some of that time will be spent trying to build motivation. You won't. You will wake up and take action, because you know it is the fastest way to build desire, and the only way to make progress.

The following chapters will teach you what kind of action to take and how to ensure that those actions achieve your goals.

Take the Action Assessment at kylebrost.com/escalate to receive personalized recommendations for achieving your goals

CHAPTER 2

Cordia Harrington – A Poignant Example of Action

"Experience is a master teacher, even when it's not our own."
– GINA GREENLEE

Keep the story of Thomas Edison in mind while we get to know an extraordinary woman named Cordia Harrington—an American entrepreneur who found great success in manufacturing, transportation, the fast-food restaurant segment, real estate, construction, and recently as a baker known affectionately as "The Bun Lady."

In this chapter, we will explore her life and her actions because she is a tremendous example of the principles laid out in this book. Throughout the rest of the book, we will reference events in her life to help you internalize what each principle looks like in practice.

This book was specifically designed to help you apply its lessons and change your life, and if it doesn't do that, you can throw it on the shelf next to the one tattered book from high school that you actually read.

Contrary to popular opinion success isn't dependent on where you've been or where you start. Those who believe that give up their influence and control. You gain influence and control by accepting that success is only dependent on where you go from here.

You can go anywhere in life from right where you are today. Take Cordia's story as just one example of how you can do that.

While at a client dinner in the fall of 2015 in a Nashville, Tennessee restaurant, I overheard a couple talking about a woman at one of the other tables. They recounted how she played a vital role at a McDonald's franchise and how at one point she had met with the brand over 30 times to accomplish a goal. I immediately wanted to know more about this action-oriented woman.

Later in the evening, I introduced myself to Cordia Harrington. Although I didn't get much time to chat with her, I stayed in touch and over the next two years I learned how impressive Cordia is. Her ability to take action, starting with the smallest methods and escalating her efforts is an example to us all.

Like most achievers, Cordia seemed about average in skills and smarts as a young woman—but she did have one major thing going for her. You can call it scrappiness, grit, or hustle, but Cordia had a knack for taking resolute action and infusing those initial actions into others.

Those who met her when she was just starting out, or when she only had a few hundred dollars to her name, knew she would be successful because she was a doer. She had moves. Simply put, she was an achiever. She wasn't afraid to take action, so she was always in motion, always moving forward, always building momentum.

Power in motion is more than good intentions. It involves more than clever ideas or piecing together resources. At its very core, it's the ability to take determined action. In essence, if you don't move, not even the best ideas will get you out of a dangerous spot. Action is crucial to making progress. And Cordia's progress is inspiring.

We can all think of ridiculous ideas that have been phenomenally successful, which is evidence that the quality of the idea is much less important than how someone acted on it. Think of the now iconic Pet Rock or the even more absurd Alex Tew's Million-Dollar Homepage, dedicated exclusively to advertisements sold at $1 per pixel. The website, which was merely a hodge-podge of ads, brought in over $1M in the first year.[3]

As the saying goes, "You can't steer a car until it's moving." For Cordia Harrington, taking action involved searching for ordinary things she could transform into extraordinary advantages. And that is precisely what she did.

Learning to Take Action

Growing up in St. Louis, Missouri, Cordia watched her father work two jobs. Her father, Mr. Barton was a salesman by day and a floor polisher by night. A trip to McDonald's was a special outing for her family, and her mother pinched pennies to buy Cordia and her two siblings a single new pair of shoes each school year. Despite all of this, Cordia says she never felt poor—only loved and driven to do better.

From an early age, Cordia's combination of desire and action was apparent. At nine, she was hosting a lemonade stand, and later she taught swimming lessons. Later, while in college, long before the advent of cell phones and selfies, she began a business photographing school kids and selling the pictures to their parents. Cordia even imported hammocks from Mexico to sell. And as she grew, so did her ambitions. With every small success inspiring more action, her progress accelerated.

Taking the skills she gained at the age of nine, she transformed a simple lemonade stand into a thriving neighborhood business. Cordia's business acuity went from strength to strength. The actions that made her successful as a child are the same ones that led to her continued success.

Many eleven-year-olds would feel timid by the idea of going door-to-door to offer their services, but not Cordia. She launched a summertime daycare business, caring for local children in her "nursery" while their parents were at work. She ran the daycare on her own, taking the initiative without any help from the grown-ups who paid her to supervise their kids.

The task was initially daunting; however, she knew if she could get the kids to her house—it would make it much easier to do.

Cordia watched the children from 9 a.m. until noon in her backyard, and for six weeks, she would walk around her neighborhood every morning to collect them. The young

Pied Piper herded the group back to her house, where the children would color, play dress-up, and delve into arts and crafts. By the end of the summer, after paying for her materials and expenses, Cordia had netted sixty dollars profit—no small feat for a kid in the 1960s!

Unbeknownst to her, Mr. Barton secretly spent some of her sixty dollars on a $5 gold piece. He held onto it until she graduated from college (Incidentally, Cordia was the first in her family to earn her degree). At the graduation ceremony, her father presented her with the gold coin; it continues to serve as a constant reminder to take action.

Bigger Actions, Bigger Results

As an adult, Cordia's life was not without challenges. She went through a divorce in 1988 and was left in debt, raising three sons under the age of seven.

"I was in survival mode, scared to death," she told People Magazine. "Many mornings driving to work, tears would be streaming down my face as I watched the sun come up." In these moments though, Cordia didn't dwell on how low she was, she recognized that she had much room to grow and that potential excited her.

And again, Cordia relied on taking action. She used her entire life savings, which amounted to $587, to start a real estate company. With little money to her name, she couldn't afford a storage unit, let alone an office. But that didn't stop Cordia from persevering.

On Main Street, Cordia found an empty office building. Where others saw a vacant building, Cordia saw an opportunity for action. She immediately contacted the owner of the building, Dr. John King, and struck a deal. If she managed to fill the structure with tenants, they would give her office space for free.

Her early ventures had taught her that she could do anything she set her mind to by taking action. And in this instance, what other choice did she have? Of course, she wasn't just peddling photographs to parents anymore; now she had to find enough tenants to fill a building and convince them it was the right space.

She persevered! Cordia filled the building and was given office space to develop her real estate business.

Cordia had no money to buy a desk or chair for her new office. Unperturbed she rented a desk for $3.50 a month and a chair for $1.75 from Burris Off Machine. With her rented furniture, she successfully grew her company.

Cordia already knew that to be successful you have to keep moving and keep taking action. Before long she took her real estate company one step further and launched a construction business. Given the scope of her determination, Cordia sold homes faster than contractors could build them. Tired of waiting for the contractors to complete the houses on time, she decided to build the structures herself by becoming a licensed contractor.

One day Cordia sold a home to a new couple in town and found out they had just purchased the local McDonald's franchise. While soaking in the hot tub at their new home, they praised Cordia for her determination and suggested that she consider buying a franchise of her own. Until she met the couple, Cordia hadn't even realized you could own a McDonald's.

That moment, Cordia decided that she too would own a McDonald's franchise. By this point, she had built a chain of action that involved capturing new opportunities. Her achievements were building, and with every action that she took, whether it proved a success or failure, she learned and applied it to the next step she decided to take.

These insights and her sheer determination allowed Cordia to buy a McDonald's franchise in rural Effingham, Illinois. Sure, she had to sell every one of her assets and borrow, to earn enough to buy the restaurant, but she calmly took one action after another until she had her McDonald's.

With the paperwork signed, Cordia figured buying a McDonald's franchise would give her more free time. At last, she could take a breather, sit back, and cash the checks. Of course, the transition was far from easy. She had to keep one business running while she journeyed to Effingham to launch a new one.

Then, four months after buying her restaurant, corporate called a meeting. In the meeting, they informed her that the effects of a war—a slow economy and government spending cuts—meant that sales were down. Subsequently, they had decided to drop the price of the brand's Value Meals from $5.99 to $2.99.

Cordia had just invested everything she had in the business, and this announcement was devastating for her. She was sure the dramatic price cut would cripple her financially. She cried the entire way home convinced she would soon go broke.

Building Momentum

In contrast to the carefree family trips to McDonald's she had taken as a child, family nights now involved cleaning the restaurant with her kids. Even with the help of her loving kids, she was still losing more than twenty thousand dollars each week and subsidized payroll costs with her own money.

As helpless as she felt, Cordia continued to search for a solution. She mused over how McDonald's was one of the most recognized brands in the world. If brand recognition and the millions corporate spent on advertising couldn't bring more customers into her restaurant, what could she possibly do?

Many would have cut their losses and moved on at this point but rather than bailing out of a struggling business, Cordia prudently considered every action available to her.

To learn more about how to identify the actions that lead directly to results visit kylebrost.com/escalate and sign up for my newsletter

The first thing Cordia did was purchase a CB radio, the kind that long-haul truckers use to communicate. Her restaurant sat on a corridor of Illinois with one interstate running north-south and another running east-west, with hundreds of trucks speeding past every day. Cordia used the radio to sell her wares, enticing passing drivers to her door with attractive food deals.

While this was far from the cash solution she needed for her predicament, it was a decisive action, and it inspired her. Cordia figured that if you can't control pricing and margins are stable, there is only one way to increase profitability, and that is to get more customers through the door.

So what would be a guaranteed way to drive more customers into the restaurant? What she needed was customers by the busload. The indomitable Cordia, of course, made it happen!

As she thought about the location of her business, Cordia spotted a lifeline, the local Greyhound bus route traveled close by. If she could alter the route to include a stop at her restaurant, she would have a captive customer base. She quickly purchased the Greyhound bus franchise for the area and rerouted the buses to include a designated stop at the parking lot outside her establishment.

Suddenly 80-120 busloads of people were frequenting her restaurant each day, and the results were phenomenal. Cordia's sales increased by over one million dollars.

This simple move allowed Cordia to turn a dramatically struggling store, into one of the top-performing McDonald's franchises in the nation. After turning her restaurant into a winner, Cordia went on to build two others.

She was one of the only woman franchisees and was quickly nominated to the McDonald's Bun Committee—a group of franchisees and McDonald's leaders who oversaw the bakeries that produced and distributed their hamburger buns.

Being on the committee gave her insight into global supply chain challenges. Given her track record for taking action,

Cordia started by learning and soaking in as much information as she could.

She put together a proposal to create a new company that could strengthen bun production, selling directly to McDonald's. Although initially reject, she was undeterred. Cordia revised and presented her plan numerous times. It took nearly 30 meetings (yes, 30!), but finally, she managed to convince McDonald's to let her build a new bakery. After selling her franchises, Cordia started the Tennessee Bun Company (now called The Bakery Cos.).

When she started her bakery, Cordia had an exclusive deal to supply McDonald's only. However, this wasn't a good long-term model for Cordia. She had to rely on lower margins and couldn't spread costs across vendors, which was unsustainable.

Again, she found herself scared and teary eyed daily. Her sales were down by 38%. Cordia struggled to pay staff members for 40 hours of work each week and was forced to cut hours and take on extra duties herself.

Cordia had to decide whether she would go broke in her current situation or create another solution. So once again, she headed to McDonald's headquarters with a new plan. It took countless meetings with McDonald's corporate, but Cordia eventually convinced them that selling to others would benefit the corporation. She suggested the company could share the fixed overhead and minimize everyone's risk, to which they finally agreed with a handshake.

The change in business model proved to be so successful that now McDonald's requires all their suppliers to use a similar protocol, which ensures McDonald's is not their only customer.

Through continued action, the keystone of Cordia's life, The Bakery Cos., has grown to produce buns for McDonald's and over 1,000 other customers. Our heroine continued to take consistent, small actions whenever a hurdle came her way.

At one point, as Cordia took on a full third of the production of the Artisan Grilled Chicken Sandwich roll in the United States, a massive piece of equipment that cost over 2 million dollars collapsed in the middle of the night. The results were catastrophic. Her production ground to a halt during a critical, national rollout.

Cordia could easily have become paralyzed by the severity of the situation, but instead, she faced up to adversity. She immediately rounded up the contact information for all the stakeholders and began making calls.

Admitting what had happened to her clients was an uncomfortable task, but she was able to reassure them she was taking action to overcome the problem. Next, she hit the phone to recruit engineers, and even chartered planes, to help fix the problem.

Her speed to address the cataclysmic situation paid off. The equipment was repaired and replaced, production reinstated, product deadlines met, and her business continued to thrive. It wasn't genius that saved the day. It was a phone call, and another, and another—constant simple action.

One thing Cordia never let get in her way was worrying about if she was taking the right action or not. She always focuses more on taking action than on whether it is the absolute correct action.

In case you fell asleep somewhere in this amazing story or want to review it again, listen to the exclusive interview with Cordia Harrington at kylebrost.com/podcast-2.

We could all learn a thing or two from her. She has never waited for someone to guide her, tell her what comes next, or outline a plan for her. No, Cordia has always known that by taking action, she will steer herself in the right direction.

Nothing can be achieved by sitting still and ruminating. There were sleepless nights and anxiety-ridden days, but Cordia understood one thing that many people do not: When the money's not there, and the love, the people, the plan, and the path are shrouded in darkness, resolute action will get the achiever through.

Courageous action was a guiding force in Cordia's career, and it continues to drive her today. It characterizes people like her and reveals that even when the odds are against you, and you don't have all the answers, you can rely on your ability to put yourself into motion.

While we have talked about how Cordia's actions largely fueled her success, we must recognize that she wouldn't become "the Bun Lady," if starved of the help of others. Without the help of her children when her franchise was failing, the encouragement of her father, or the initial investment by various people who believed in her, she could not have made it to where she is today.

You, like Cordia, will need help along the way. To ask for and receive is not weakness but strength. Getting the help you need to escalate your work is a principle we will talk about later in this book.

Learning from this, Cordia has always strived to be a mentor and model of service. To date, she has helped 17 former employees become McDonald's owner-operators and, subsequently, millionaires. Out of all the success we've covered in Cordia's life, she views this as a blessing and one of her greatest accomplishments.

CHAPTER 3

Take Action Today to Ensure You Act Tomorrow

"Every body continues in its state of rest, or of uniform motion in a right line, unless it is compelled to change that state by forces impressed upon it."

–SIR ISAAC NEWTON

As Newton discovered, "an object at rest stays at rest and an object in motion stays in motion." The same goes for you.

The old mentality that you should wait until you are motivated to do anything is destructive. While you wait for motivation, time passes, and productivity is lost.

Humans are incredible procrastinators and this old mentality encourages procrastination and slows progress. When you're too focused on doing one task, you ignore all of the other available tasks.

When this happens take any action to move you forward, even if that action is seemingly unrelated to your goal.

Taking any meaningful action is one thousand times more inspiring and productive than waiting and procrastinating.

It is impossible to predict what your own map of achievement will look like in 10 years. But, even if the results of your actions are unpredictable, there are other reasons action matters. That is, aside from the obvious that it is the only way to make progress. As you have seen, action enables learning and iteration. Action also perpetuates action. It is inspiring and reinforcing.

Repeat that: Action perpetuates action. You don't admire achievers because they have accomplished a single grand thing and are never heard from again; you respect them because they continue to take action and achieve great things.

I wouldn't be championing Cordia's story if she had stopped taking action after merely running her nursery, or after building a modestly successful real estate company. I share her story and the stories of other achievers because they continue to take action. It is their persistence that is admirable.

ANYONE CAN GET THEMSELVES TO TAKE ONE SIMPLE ACTION, BUT IT'S THOSE WHO REPEAT THE PROCESS COUNTLESS TIMES THAT WE HOLD UP AS EXAMPLES.

This kind of person has discovered the secret that action perpetuates action...even if the actions are unrelated.

Are you more productive on the day you sleep in and rush off to work? Or are you more productive when you wake up on a schedule and exercise first? The second option is much closer to reality, even when working out is unrelated to what you do at work.

In her bestselling book, *The Life-Changing Magic Of Tidying Up*, Marie Kondo reveals how clients who take action to declutter their homes often report experiencing other life successes soon after, including weight loss and improved work focus.[4] This is because action perpetuates action, even if the actions are unrelated.

To benefit from the momentum building effect of action, it doesn't need to be directly related to your goal. So, act now! No matter how small the effort, a little action is always better than nothing at all. The importance of taking seemingly insignificant action cannot be underestimated, for it is small actions that lead to bigger ones.

Remember how action plus desire equals progress? Well, it's not just that action and design add up to progress, the two also strengthen each other. One of the greatest myths is that desire always precedes action. It does not. Acting can come before desire and will in fact increase your desire. The two reinforce each other.

Consider how many times you lacked desire, but because of obligation, pressure, or a deadline you did it anyway. Also consider how many times after starting, you found it was easy to keep going. This is because action perpetuates action.

Taking a small, simple action is far easier than convincing yourself that you need an arbitrary level of desire before you can start. You don't have to lead with desire, you can lead with action, so remember Action + Desire = Progress.

The Immeasurable Value of Small Tasks

The following is a short excerpt from the remarks of Naval Admiral William H. McRaven, ninth commander of the U.S. Special Operations Command, at the university-wide Commencement at the University of Texas, Austin on May 17, 2014:[5]

> Every morning in basic SEAL training, my instructors, who at the time were all Vietnam veterans, would show up in my barracks room and the first thing they would inspect was your bed. If you did it right, the corners would be square, the covers pulled tight, the pillow centered just under the headboard and the extra blanket folded neatly at the foot of the rack — that's Navy talk for bed.
>
> It was a simple task — mundane at best. But every morning we were required to make our bed to perfection. It seemed a little ridiculous at the time, particularly in light of the fact that we were aspiring to be real warriors, tough battle-hardened SEALs, but the wisdom of this simple act has been proven to me many times over.
>
> If you make your bed every morning you will have accomplished the first task of the day. It will give you a small sense of pride, and it will encourage you to do another task and another and another. By the end of the day, that one task completed will have turned into many tasks completed. Making your bed will also reinforce the fact that little things in life matter. If you can't do the little things right, you will never do the big things right.

> And, if by chance you have a miserable day, you will come home to a bed that is made — that you made — and a made bed gives you encouragement that tomorrow will be better.
>
> If you want to change the world, start off by making your bed.

The strengthening and perpetuating effects of action are not limited to the short-term. Action can have a culminating impact across a lifetime, and the sooner and more often you take action, the more action you will take throughout your life.

We have already examined how the actions Cordia Harrington took as a child, and later as a single mother, enabled her to develop the confidence she needed to solve problems. By taking consistent action over the years, she learned to experience failure and move beyond it. That is the power of taking action; it unlocks your ability to keep on moving and learn from your mistakes. Without action, this ability remains locked away.

Cordia's early experiences of turning multiple actions into success undoubtedly prepared her to take initiative to bring in customers by the busload, change McDonald's approach to working with suppliers, fix a disaster in the middle of a national rollout, and continue to create paths to future goals.

While others procrastinate the one task on their list, you shift your focus to another meaningful tasks that you will get done. Through this simple shift, you will make more progress in an hour, than ten procrastinators focused on a single task will in a day.

There is no better way to gain great insights and capabilities for success than to take action. Because action will teach you along the way, you don't need to map out every detail of your journey beforehand. You can build your map along the way.

Quick Tips:

1. *Make small commitments to yourself. Rather than starting with a big goal in mind, taking action can start with small commitments to yourself. Commit to reflect for 5 minutes a day, wake up 5 minutes earlier, or spend 5 minutes on a habit you've been wanting to develop. As soon as you complete your small commitment, make another one.*

2. *Write about goals and plans regularly. The power writing has to produce action has been proven repeatedly. As an initial step, write 2-3 sentences about your goals and plans every single day.*

3. *Take action first thing in the morning and the last thing at night. Start your day with a small and simple action that matters to you and end your day the same way. Whether it's making your bed, meditating, or 50 sit-ups, start and end your day with action.*

CHAPTER 4

Don't Look for a Map, Build Your Own Along the Way

"Do not go where the path may lead, go instead where there is no path and leave a trail."

– RALPH WALDO EMERSON

Analysts say you should spend the majority of your time planning and preparing. The problem? Things rarely go according to plan. As the controversial boxer Mike Tyson used to say, "Everyone has a plan until they get punched in the mouth".

The better way is to focus on executing and adapting. In this way you can map your course as you move forward through effort.

How much effort would it take to travel from New York City to Hong Kong, before locomotives, automobiles, or airplanes? Well, from 1804 to 1806, two men led an expedition across the western United States. They covered more than 8,000 miles, the equivalent of going from New York City to Hong Kong. However, rather than planning their trip, Meriwether Lewis and William Clark let their actions drive them forward.

At the request of President Thomas Jefferson, Lewis and Clark set out to explore the Louisiana Territory, the land west of the Mississippi purchased from France in 1803. Lewis was Jefferson's personal secretary, and the president believed his organization and strength would help him navigate the rocky terrain of the American West. Ensign Meriwether Lewis had served under Clark in the Kentucky Militia. The two developed a strong friendship that carried through to their exploration.

So, Lewis and Clark began their travels near St. Louis, Missouri, in May 1804. They were eager to discover unfamiliar places, make peace with the Native American tribes they encountered, and share their findings.

They prepared 140 maps directly on the trail, in response to their environment, and secured another 30 from Native Americans, fur trappers, and traders on their trek.[6] Like Cordia Harrington's entrepreneurial journey, they forged their own path—and the results were extraordinary.

Thomas Edison charted his course through 9,000 failures, each one a new point of reference on his map of action. Surely, he added to his lessons learned from those who learned before him, just as Lewis and Clark added to their own created maps, thirty from those who went before them. As you map your own course through action, don't neglect to learn from those who have gone before.

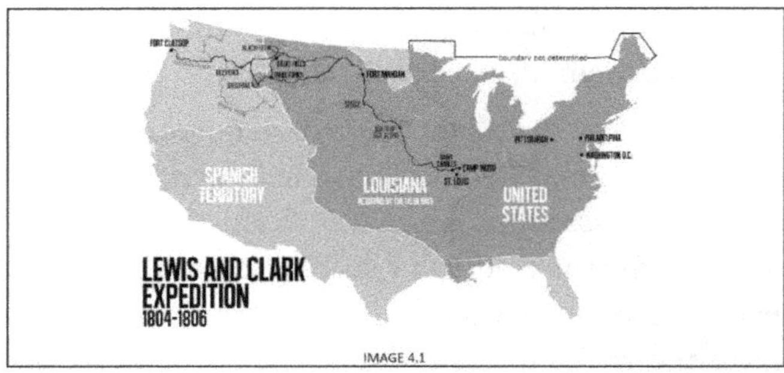

IMAGE 4.1

Referred to as the Corps of Discovery, the explorers traveled through tumultuous weather, illness, and injury. Despite the adversity met, they did not once consider ending their expedition early. Over three years, they journeyed nearly eight thousand miles in the name of westward expansion and diplomacy. Even when Lewis was robbed in 1806 and shot by one of his men in a hunting accident, the Corps of Discovery made good on their promise to explore the frontier.

While their first winter proved difficult, the explorers took a series of actions that set the tone for the rest of their expedition. They treated Mandan, a Native American Tribe of the Great Plains (now North Dakota) with respect, and as a result, earned the trust of Sacagawea, a Shoshone Indian.

She and her husband Toussaint Charbonneau traveled for thousands of miles to steer them in the right direction during difficult times.[7] By thinking on their feet, taking action, and forging their own maps, Lewis and Clark—like Cordia Harrington on her journey—achieved the unimaginable.

As you take action throughout life, you will lead a personal Corps of Discovery. You cannot analyze your way to a perfect map, so focus on what you are discovering along the way and capture the lessons learned to increase your future successes.

EVERY DISCOVERY, ACHIEVEMENT, AND FAILURE WILL BE A NEW POINT CHARTED ON YOUR COURSE.

A Tale of Life-Saving Action

Oscar Hechter, an award-winning doctor whose research helped shape modern endocrinology science, shared this story about getting into motion in an extreme situation during the First World War.[8]

It begins with a platoon commander sending a squad of Hungarian troops, who had been camping in the Alps, out on a scouting mission.

Shortly after the group left camp, it began to snow, and the storm continued for two days. The scouting squad did not return, and guilt struck the young officer. In his despair, he questioned not only the scouting mission, but the war itself, and his role in the conflict. He was a tormented man.

Suddenly, on the third day, the long-overdue scouting squad returned sparking great joy throughout the camp.

“Where were you?” the young commander asked with relief. “How did you survive? How did you find your way back?”

“We were lost in the snow and had given up hope," explained the sergeant in charge of the group. "We had resigned ourselves to die, but then one of the men found a map in his pocket. With its help, we knew we could find our way back. We made camp, waited for the snow to stop, and then as soon as we could travel, we returned here."

The young commander asked to see the map. Upon close examination, he found it was not a map of the Alps, but another French mountain range, the Pyrenees!

The lieutenant was amazed. It wasn’t the map that had got his men out of trouble; it was the action the map had spurred. It hadn't done much in the way of guiding them back to camp, but it had given the troop the strength of will to get moving. It had given them the hope to stay calm, wait out the storm, and focus on their safe return.

The young commander looked at his men and concluded that taking an action was more important than taking the right action.

TAKING ACTION IS FAR MORE EFFECTIVE THAN OVER-ANALYZING WHETHER IT IS THE RIGHT ACTION

When individuals worry more about if they are taking the right action than they do about taking an action, they are immediately at risk of getting stuck.

This can be seen in both our stories. If Lewis and Clark hadn't embarked with incomplete information, someone else would be famous, and if our Hungarian troops hadn't used a faulty map to give them the courage to press forward, they'd be dead in the snow.

Maybe you worry about whether you're taking the right action and find yourself stuck as a result. This feeling is often called paralysis by analysis. It happens when you get so focused on eliminating every risk that you fail to take even a single step forward.

Your effort to analyze every possible action has paralyzed your ability to take action.

Taking the right action is far less important than just taking action. Richard Branson is famous for his "screw it, let's do it" attitude that encourages people to start before they are ready.

The truth is that you will rarely feel prepared to take action, but if you don't act, you inherently question your decisions. Besides, readiness is best evaluated in hindsight. Even with all the analysis in the world, the only sure way to know if it will work is to try.

Some of your associates are stuck because they are trying to map out every detail of the path ahead. They spend 90% of their time preparing and only 10% taking action. The problem is that they can never predict nor be prepared for everything, so their course will change regardless.

You, on the other hand, see the power of getting started, emphasizing action over a perfect map. You make progress today knowing that the only way to create an accurate map is to navigate it.

Whether the perfect action or not, taking action puts you in places to discover new things, identify opportunities, and to learn.

Once you start mapping your journey, you'll feel inspired to keep going, even if your direction isn't perfectly clear. And this inspiration will only grow as you continue moving forward.

Quick Tips:

1. *Start with what's easy. To take action, start with what comes easily to you, by doing this, you'll get into motion and be able to map your course. The key is to consistently look for how what you're already doing can be connected to bigger goals.*

2. *Balance analysis with action. When you overanalyze your goal or the right action, it can become overwhelming—balance this analysis with taking action. A good rule of thumb is 20% analysis and 80% action. If you can't take any action because of analysis, you're overanalyzing.*

3. *Receive feedback along the way. It's one thing to move forward without a map, it's another to move forward carelessly. While you may not know the route you'll take today, you should receive feedback along the way to improve the course you're on. Without this, you won't actually be mapping your course, you'll just be wandering.*

CHAPTER 5

Leverage Your Most Powerful Tool, Progress

"Success is steady progress toward one's personal goals." –

–JIM ROHN

One of the reasons that action leads to more action is that with action you begin to see results. You act when you have the desire, but you also gain the desire when you act. Especially when you see the results of your actions.

This is in contrast to the old belief that a big compelling goal was enough to get you moving. A big goal without progress is less inspiring than a small goal coupled with progress.

Have you ever started a project that you didn't want to do, but then as you saw progress and results, it compelled you to keep going? I can think of many times this has been the case for me. Yard work is a prime example. We have two acres of grass and when it comes time to cut the grass, I rarely have the desire. However, once I get started and see the results, I gain the desire to keep going.

In fact, there have been several times writing this book that I have lacked the desire to write. But once I start and see the words add up and the pages grow, my desire to keep going grows.

Something as simple as a checklist can help you see the effects of your action and recognize progress. For action to increase desire, it helps to make your progress visible.

The power of visible progress has been recognized for a long time. Consider how the video game industry has used progress bars, achievement badges, and new levels as a visual reminder of progress for decades. They know that when you see your progress, you are more likely to keep going.

Why? Because visualizing your progress is powerful. So powerful in fact, that it helps a population for whom progress can be incredibly difficult to see.

Alcoholics Anonymous supports individuals for whom progress can be phenomenally difficult, and they understand the value of making progress visible. Participants work to overcome strong addictions through a 12-step program. For every stage of progress, participants receive "AA Chips" or sobriety coins.

These coins serve as a visible reminder of the individual's progress. The AA 12-step program is internationally recognized and this simple, yet powerful symbol of progress starts with receipt of a white coin for 24 hours of sobriety.

And, as Cordia Harrington received a five-dollar gold piece from her father after graduation, you too can carry reminders of the steps you're taking and your successes. These reminders of your progress and achievements will give you the desire to keep going.

In your own life, the way you make progress visible should be meaningful—it should speak to you on a personal level—whether you choose to make a list, hang a plaque with your achievements, or just carry a five-dollar gold coin.

To reinforce the importance of visible progress, let's look at a study performed by Dan Ariely, the renowned professor of psychology and behavioral economics at Duke University.[9] He studied students who were paid to build Lego models.

Each model was composed of forty pieces and accompanied by instructions, with only one way for the Legos to be assembled. The students were paid for every figurine they built.

In one group, each completed model was placed on the desk in front of the students. The students would then receive another box and start assembling the next model. With every model set on the counter, the students' progress was visible.

Alternatively, in another group, the students received two boxes. Every time they completed a model, it was at once dismantled and placed back in the box, so the students could start assembling the second box. In this latter group, they continually cycled through the two boxes, assembling and reassembling the same models.

This condition is often called the Sisyphus Condition, named after the King of Ephyra from Greek mythology, who was forced to roll an immense boulder up a hill—only to watch it come back and crush him. For this reason, futile efforts are frequently called Sisyphean.

It's important to note that in both groups, all of the models were identical, so there was no more variety in one group than the other. The first group, whose actions were visible, outperformed the second group **eleven to seven**. The mere fact that their progress was visible inspired them. As a result, they continued to build enthusiastically, despite being paid less for each later model.

These numbers may not seem remarkable at first glance, but they take on new meaning when you realize that the group whose progress was visible outperformed their counterparts whose progress was not by over 57%! How many organizations and individuals do you know who would pay phenomenal amounts to gain 57% more productivity?

WHAT COULD YOU ACCOMPLISH IF YOU COULD GET 57% MORE PRODUCTIVITY OUT OF YOURSELF?

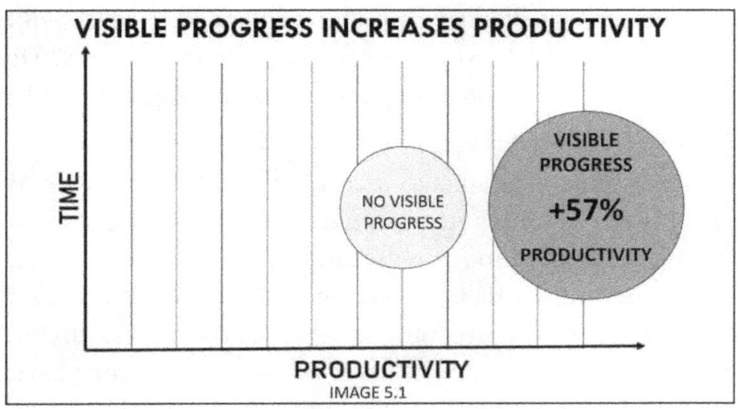

IMAGE 5.1

How do you make your actions visible? How do you find the power to take action, and gain desire from the effort you've taken? It is one thing to tell yourself that you've worked hard at the end of the day; it is another to identify what you actually did.

For action and progress to be visible and motivating, you want to engage in honest observation and reflection. If you think about and track your efforts in ambiguous terms, it will not do much for you and won't help to increase your desire. You will thrive on the visible results you see through honest observation and reflection.

The students whose progress was not visible would likely say they were working just as hard as the first group. In fact, they may even report that they were working harder because it took more effort to continue building without tangible signs of progress.

We empathize with Sisyphus because we can imagine how demoralizing it must be to work so hard achieving something and, in the end, not see any progress. Yet, how many times have you let your stone roll back down the hill because you didn't work to recognize your progress? Or because you were too ambiguous in what progress would look like?

If you want your actions to increase your desire, you need to remove the ambiguity and get specific about what you did and how it led to (or will lead to) your desired results. It is more motivating to reflect on each of your efforts and observe how they are moving you forward than to tell yourself that you "worked hard." Many people work hard every day of their lives, and yet they still lose desire.

Tell us!

There are many ways to make your actions visible. What do you do?
Share with fellow Escalators in the Escalate Facebook Group

https://www.facebook.com/groups/escalateprocess

Subtlety in Results – A Leadership Example

This could be you—you're in motion but are losing desire because you don't feel any closer to accomplishing your goal. Sometimes when you're taking small actions toward a specific purpose, it's hard to see the progress you've made.

Carrie, a well-educated and experienced client of mine, was tasked with helping her growing organization in food production implement a leadership development program. Not long into the engagement, Carrie expressed frustration about not making any progress.

"What would make you feel better about the situation?" I asked.

"Having the program in place and running," she replied.

We then walked through all the progress she had made.

"Carrie, you began this project about six months ago," I told her. "When you started, how much did you know about leadership development?"

"Nothing," she replied.

"What do you have in place right now that you didn't have in place six months ago?" I asked.

“Nothing! That’s the problem,” Carrie said dejectedly.

“You really believe you don’t have anything new in place?” I responded. Followed by, “What would you need in place right now to feel like you’ve made progress?”

“We would be offering training quarterly, have leadership development built into our performance management process, and have a suite of tools and resources for the organization to use,” she replied.

I considered her reply for a moment, “I see. Well I know for sure you have done some things. Forget what you believe you should have in place and tell me what you do have in place.”

“Well, we have three ongoing lecture series,” she said. “And we’re starting to include leadership suggestions in our newsletter and have revised some job descriptions.”

Carrie paused before reeling off several other initiatives that were also in action. I questioned her about all the steps she had taken to accomplish each achievement. There were many, including diligent efforts to find good presenters for the lecture series.

“And who did all of that?” I asked.

“I did,” she replied.

“How do you feel about your progress now, considering none of it existed just six months ago?” I questioned.

She was humbled, but also excited. "You're right," she agreed. "We have made progress. Imagine how much progress we'll make in the next six months!"

With this fresh perspective, she recognized that the organization had made tremendous advances in the six months she had worked with them. Seeing her progress began by recognizing her small efforts for what they were, small wins.

As I did with Carrie, you can recognize and reward your own progress by unpacking what you've done into the tasks it took to do it. When you focus on creating an entire leadership development program, researching presenters may not seem like a small win, but it certainly is. It has to be done, and once it is, you are one step closer to your desired results. Identify and then celebrate these things as the wins they are. Reward yourself!

Sometimes the most straightforward action can have a profound effect. Remember when Cordia's machine collapsed in the middle of a national rollout? Making that first call to her stakeholders didn't seem like it was going to solve her massive problem, but it was that first call that got her in motion and guided her toward a comprehensive solution. A single action might not seem like much, but the cumulative effect of dozens of small actions cannot be ignored.

Too often you stop yourself from taking action because you know you won't achieve your long-term goal right away. You fail to recognize that the culminating effects of small steps are what lead to extraordinary achievement.

One of the most significant issues I have run into in my work is that individuals have a tough time recognizing small wins. They focus so much on the goal, on a few large milestones, that they fail to acknowledge the progress they are making in simple ways every day.

When you fail to recognize these small wins, you miss out on a huge opportunity to gain desire and accelerate your progress.

Why Progress Matters

Teresa Amabile from the Harvard Business School calls the motivating effect of action the *Progress Principle,* in her book by the same name. She and her colleagues discovered that nothing has a more powerful impact on desire and action than making progress on meaningful work.[10]

Her research is closely related to the work of David McClelland and J.W. Atkinson on the theory of achievement motivation.[11] Which states that the desire to achieve is an innate human characteristic, and the more you see yourself moving toward achievement, the more compelled you are to continue making progress.

The exciting thing about this desire is that it does not need big wins to receive the benefits.

IN FACT, REGULAR SMALL GAINS HAVE THE SAME MOTIVATING OUTCOMES.

The only way to achieve these small victories is by taking consistent action, which is itself a small win.

Making progress visible is about recognizing the efforts you've carried out, whereas the progress principle is about recognizing how those actions have moved you toward your goal.

The opposite is also true. When you don't make progress, you lose massive amounts of desire to keep going. One of the biggest barriers to getting started and gaining momentum is exerting some effort but feeling like you haven't made any progress.

A challenge you will face at some point is the ability to recognize your progress. A young and determined employee of mine named Tyler, who was working on public speaking skills, was frustrated by his lack of progress. As he expressed his frustration to me, I sat perplexed.

While Tyler struggled to see his own progress, I could easily recognize improvements he had made. One simple improvement he had made was to drastically reduce the number of "um's." When I mentioned this, he admitted that he had improved on this, but just didn't feel like it was a big enough change.

By itself, it wasn't a big enough change to accomplish his goal, but it was without a doubt progress. Sometimes you are the last person to recognize your own progress because you are closest to it.

As you act, you will see yourself getting closer to your target. In a sense, you begin to smell, taste, and even feel the success of achievement with every step closer. When you get closer, not only do these senses get stronger but your desire to achieve grows.

That will not happen, though, if you don't make your progress visible. One way to boost this effect is to map out small victories toward your goal. By unpacking your goal, you make it manageable, and by mapping small victories, you make it inspiring.

As part of the unpacking process, also consider what some small victories would be. Think of these as quick wins that will inspire you to keep acting.

How many people do you know who are waiting to build up desire in order to take action? They rely on this slow and unpredictable process. You, however, take action in order to build up desire, this way you're making progress regardless. And, you are inspired when you make progress visible!

Quick Tips:

1. *Make your progress visible. You can make your progress visible in many ways, this can be simple like a checklist where once you complete a task, you cross it off. Nonetheless, you should create some way for you to physically see your progress.*

2. *Focus on tasks completed, not outcomes. When it comes to progress, it's all about what you've done, not about the outcomes. Outcomes are unpredictable, so focus on what tasks you have completed.*

3. *Respect the tiny things. Don't get discouraged because you didn't accomplish a huge task. Did you do something tiny that moved you forward? That is progress, and you have to acknowledge it as such.*

CHAPTER 6

Strive for Potential, Not Validation

"Progress lies not in enhancing what is, but in advancing toward what will be."

– KHALIL GIBRAN

The actions you take are directly related to the progress you make, and more importantly to the person you become. Consider that for a moment, who are you becoming? As you consider who you can become, remind yourself, it is better to become than to be.

You know others who are trying to prove their worth through performance, only concerned with validating themselves. The problem is that any sign of failure becomes massive discouragement. You, however, focus on your potential and progress, seeing gaps as inspiring opportunities for growth.

Not everyone values what they learn from their decisions; they fear failure and cannot fathom how they would ever recover from a setback. But, it's important to value what you are becoming more than who you think you are. Like Cordia Harrington, view your setbacks not as evidence of who you are not, but as signs of future potential.

Stanford University psychologist Carol S. Dweck, Ph.D., dubs this state-of-mind as the difference between a fixed and a growth mindset in her book titled, *Mindset*.[12]

In simple terms, to find power in what you are becoming, recognize the progress you are making rather than seeking validation. When you believe things about yourself that are associated with outcomes, when the outcomes are not successful you think you are a failure. People with this belief may not put themselves in a position of struggle because if failure occurs, they see it as evidence that they are a failure.

This mindset fails to recognize that failure is a momentary experience, not a person.

In turn, when you believe that you will learn and grow from your mistakes, you find power and value in them. Rather than becoming demoralized because of failure, you are inspired to grow.

The underlying question here is "How much faith do you have in yourself?"—which is another way to look at it. If you know the outcome, you do not need faith in yourself. In fact, when you are certain of the outcome, it quickly becomes routine or habit.

Really think about that for a moment. Taking action is an act of faith in yourself. You don't need a map outlining the entire journey, you just need enough direction to get you started and enough faith in yourself to take the first few steps.

With the first step you express faith in yourself. Faith that you can, with continued action, make up the difference between who you are today and who you want to be in the future. When you don't express faith in yourself by taking action, you are forced to acknowledge that you have reached your full potential.

HOW DEPRESSING WOULD IT BE IF, AT THIS STAGE IN YOUR LIFE, YOU HAD ALREADY REACHED YOUR FULL POTENTIAL?

I assure you, you have not! Find joy in the fact that outcomes do not reflect your potential. Failure indicates that you still have more to achieve—and that's exhilarating!

Correspondingly, just as failed outcomes do not make you a failure, positive results do not make you a success. Your perception should be shaped more by your effort than the outcomes of those efforts. While you can control efforts (action), you cannot control outcomes. As a result, this mindset enables you to take chances, push yourself, and ultimately learn from any failure.

With the alternative mindset, there is little growth and no desire to try something new. Instead, you think to yourself: I failed, and I am therefore a failure. Why try again? This mindset can be especially damaging if you ruminate on circumstances over which you have no control.

Take, for example, the near-disaster at Cordia's bakery. She could have beaten herself up over the burden of the collapse and convinced herself that she should have prevented it. But instead, Cordia took action and helped to solve the problem. The collapse had nothing to do with Cordia's abilities, and she focused on progress more than she did on outcomes.

This mindset encouraged Cordia to see the traumatic experience as an opportunity to take action rather than admit defeat. To this day, Cordia says she does not dwell on any failure she's experienced because she's learned something from all the missteps, mishaps, and mistakes she's faced. These struggles have taught her a great deal about success and encouraged her to persevere.

It is no coincidence that achievers have a mindset that drives them to learn from failure and continually push themselves. You might think that Cordia would slow down now that she runs a nine-figure company, but her desire is to continue progressing. Her desire to become keeps her moving forward. It pushes her to advance and improve persistently.

Your actions are shaped by your thoughts, and in these actions, you anticipate either positive or negative outcomes. Those who focus on what they are becoming are better able to embrace failure and still take action because they know the results of their actions will not define who they are.

In actuality, you should be more concerned when you are not experiencing some degree of failure. Lack of failure indicates that your progress is stalled or your goals are too small. Overall, if you consistently take action, then missteps serve as evidence that you are learning, growing, and improving.

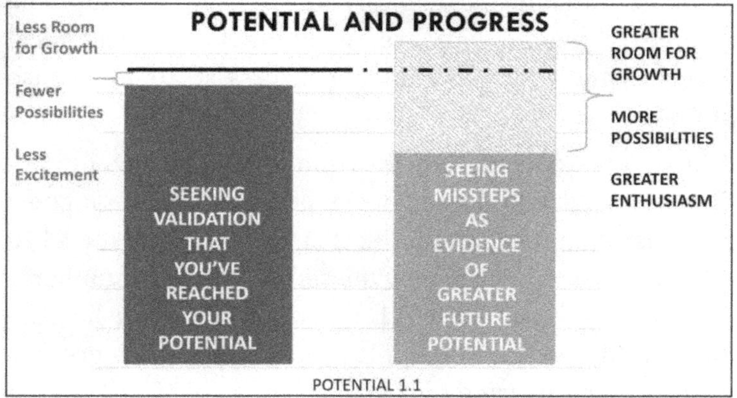

POTENTIAL 1.1

Your focus should be on taking risks that play to your strengths—risks that are within reach. And even if you fail, you can acknowledge what you've learned, get back up, dust yourself off, and try again. You might experience 9,000 missteps, but when you persist, those 9,000 missteps will turn you into an action powerhouse.

Failure versus Potential

In 1998 a brazen man pieced together $12,000. With it, he rented a theatre in Atlanta, hoping to sell out his play *I Know I've Been Changed*. If he sold the 1200 seats, he would make $20,000. But, that's not how it went, within weeks he was penniless and homeless. He had failed. Should he take that failure as an indicator of his potential? Did this failure mean he was doomed as an actor, director, and producer? Or, was his failure evidence of how much room he had to grow?

Tyler Perry took his failure as an opportunity to grow. Rather than becoming demoralized and quitting, he recognized that he had a lot of room to grow. And grow he did. Perry pushed forward, peddling his play at local churches and eventually finding success at Atlanta House of Blues.

If he had taken his failure to mean he had no potential in film, he would have missed out on becoming Forbes highest paid man in entertainment in 2011, when he made $130 million. He would have also missed out on four number 1 films and sales of over 11 million DVDs.[13] As he said himself, "All you can do is plant your seed in the ground, water it every day and believe."

When you look at success in others and in your own life, you'll see the theme of potential surface time and time again. WD-40 was the 40th attempt to create a degreaser and rust protection solvent, and Dyson tested 5,271 prototypes before finding a design that worked.

How many failures on your way to achievement have you experienced? Just like these examples, your achievement is just on the other side of challenge and repetition because achievement is your potential.

Your potential is yours alone. Don't rely on the potential you see in others. When you do this, you limit yourself to incremental improvements. When you aspire to only be like someone else, there is limited improvement to make. However, when you challenge the very foundation of who you are personally, you discover endless possibility.

Do you see failure as evidence of who you are or who you can become? Are you striving to be the person deep down you know only you can be?

The old way was to validate yourself, so you could prove to others your worth. This approach prohibits growth. The new way, the way you approach each day, is to focus on your potential and what you are becoming. By doing this, you will wake everyday with a sense of possibility.

Quick Tips:

1. *Shift your mindset. Before all else, you must shift your mindset about what gaps in your performance really mean. Until you can see gaps as opportunities and appreciate the blessing of growth, you will seek out validation. Every time you catch yourself seeking validation, pause and begin looking for opportunity.*

2. *Stop comparing and contrasting. One of the biggest barriers to recognizing potential is when you constantly compare and contrast yourself against others. No matter how wealthy, sexy, or intelligent you are, there will always be someone who in comparison will make you feel not so. You must stop comparing yourself to what you believe others are and start comparing yourself to what you believe you can be.*

3. *Forgive yourself and others. Until you forgive yourself for mistakes and shortcomings, you'll be caught up in despair and have a hard time*

appreciating your potential. Accept that no matter how many goals you achieve, you'll never be perfect, and you'll always have room to grow. This is true for others as well. Forgive yourself and others so that you can move forward without the burden.

CHAPTER

Be Undaunted from the Start

"Doubt kills more dreams than failure ever will."

– SUZY KASSEM

Accelerating progress is one thing, but simply getting started can be daunting. Especially, when you stand at the foot of your mountain-like goal looking up at the peak. That lofty goal can suddenly appear overwhelming, too much for you to accomplish.

However, you can make it feel doable by breaking it down into small tasks and goals. This is known as *unpacking* because you are unpacking your big goal into a series of manageable activities.

Some believe you must take massive action to achieve big goals. The problem is that no one knows what qualifies as massive action. So, these individuals stall while they try to identify that one massive action that will propel them forward. They are looking for a silver bullet.

You're not looking for silver bullet actions, because you know that all great achievements are achieved through small actions. You create big goals but focus on small actions. This way you have confidence to take those first few steps forward, no matter how big the goal.

Always remember, the goals you set must be big, but the actions you take must be small.

From where you are today, climbing to the peak of your mountain of a goal might seem impossible. The fear of falling short can be demoralizing and strip you of any desire to take action and move forward. However, if you break down the effort required to scale the mountain into all of its components, and focus on each one individually, it becomes manageable. It becomes possible.

You may not be able to climb to the top of the mountain today, but how can you prepare for that epic journey? Can you work out what you need and break down the steps to get there?

You see, each of those small steps gets you a little closer to the summit. And cumulatively, when you add up enough small steps, you will be at the summit. So, when you unpack big things into small tasks and then focus on those little things, it is exciting because those small things are very doable.

BIG GOALS 1.1

This becomes a reinforcing process. By focusing on something small, and knowing you can achieve it today, you have the desire and excitement to do it. Then, once you do it, you have a visible display of your progress, which excites you even more.

EXTRAORDINARY IS MORE A RESULT THAN IT IS A BEHAVIOR;

IT IS THE RESULT OF REPEATED AND SUSTAINED ORDINARY BEHAVIOR.

Often, getting yourself excited and eager to take action simply requires a different perspective. It requires taking something grand and visionary, and unpacking it into smaller, more practical steps that you can work on immediately. And then, by rewarding yourself for progress made through small actions, you can generate even more remarkable results.

This process of breaking a large intimidating goal into smaller more manageable goals is called unpacking. You will learn this specific process in Section 2 of this book.

The concern that sometimes gets expressed is that those small tasks don't seem very compelling. Don't lose the forest through the trees, meaning, don't lose sight of the fact that your goal will be accomplished through those small and simple steps. Learn that extraordinary is more a result than it is a behavior. It is the result of repeated and sustained ordinary behavior. Summiting a mountain is the result—the result of putting one foot in front of the other, repeatedly.

As you become adept at completing the small and simple tasks, you become better at completing the big ones. However, you will never be able to eliminate the ordinary tasks that produce extraordinary results.

Barry Finlay, who at 60 had never climbed a mountain before, decided to summit Mt. Kilimanjaro.[14] After completing this goal, and transforming his career and life, he said, "Every mountain top is within reach, if you just keep climbing." After coming down from the summit, Barry became an author and philanthropist.

He was not only able to summit Mt. Kilimanjaro but start a new career that has produced five award-winning books. All of this was due to one simple thing, his ability to take a very large goal and unpack it into the small and simple steps needed to achieve it.

In 2016, I had my own experience in summiting a peak and I wasn't alone. My son, who was five years old at the time, and I decided we would summit the second highest peak in the continental United States.

At 14,439 feet it felt like an insurmountable goal to my five-year-old son—and at times throughout the journey, it felt like one to me as well! However, we talked throughout our seven and a half hour climb to the summit about what our next goal would be.

Instead of constantly focusing on the summit, which at times we couldn't even see, we would pick small goals that we knew we could achieve. For example, we would commit to hiking for 10 minutes before stopping again, or we would pick a point ahead on the trail to reach.

Inch by inch, goal by goal, we made our way up the summit. I could not possibly count how many small goals we set for ourselves that day, but ultimately those small goals, those achievable milestones, were what enabled us to succeed.

By unpacking our big goal into small manageable goals, we were able to reach the summit. My five-year-old was by far the youngest person on the mountain that day, and he was able to achieve his goal through the simple process of unpacking.

SMALL STEPS TO ACHIEVEMENT

BIG GOALS 1.2

You can use unpacking in amazing ways. Take Kyle Korver for example. An American player in the National Basketball

Association, he unpacked the perfect jump shot into a 20-point checklist.[15]

By unpacking his jump shot into 20 different elements, he can focus on specific pieces when his shot is off. Rather than trying to focus on something that's too big and too ambiguous like, "just shoot smoother." He can focus on things like wide stance, exaggerated legs, slight bend at waist, fingers spread, or slight pause.

Do you see how much easier and more effective it is to focus on those small components of the bigger whole? It matters, and it works. By unpacking his jump shot into its smaller components, Kyle Korver went on to break the record for single season 3-Point field goal percentage in the 2009-2010 season. His record of .5364 percent for the season stands today as the highest 3-Point percentage in NBA history.

Don't fall into the old trap of believing massive action is the route to success. The route to achieving your goals is through small and simple actions repeated over time.

The principle of unpacking your big goal into small actions, will help you get started and make progress. Apply the principles now to start and read on to learn how to build lifelong momentum.

Quick Tips:

1. *Make your goal clear. You'll find it difficult to unpack a goal that is ambiguous and unclear. If you want to break a big goal down into manageable parts, first get very clear and specific about what that goal is in practical and measurable terms.*

2. *Try timelines. If you struggle to unpack your goal by tasks, try unpacking it by timelines. What can you accomplish in 30 days? 3 months? 6 months? By focusing on timelines, you can identify what you already believe you can accomplish realistically.*

3. *Use what you're already doing. Rather than starting from scratch with a big list of activities, you can also start with what you're already doing. Identify those daily activities you already do that can help move you toward your goal, then build on those by strengthening their connection to your goal. For example, do you already journal daily? Try journaling about your goal. Do you already plan with your calendar? Try adding a goal component to your daily schedule.*

CHAPTER 8

Learn the Essentials of Building Momentum

"To advance, however far, is profitless unless the ground gained can be consolidated, or the momentum sustained."

– LUDOVIC KENNEDY

Getting started on a big goal is different than building lifelong momentum. As you become an action powerhouse, you will build momentum.

Too many people consider each goal in isolation and ignore what they are becoming. The problem is that what they are becoming has a profound impact on their future goals. Your way is to focus on what you're becoming, this way you can build momentum with every goal, including your future ones.

Have you ever noticed how so many of the successful people you know, keep achieving more? And how their success in one area of life often transfers to other areas?

Take Cordia Harrington for example, she didn't stop at teaching kids, selling real estate, or running a McDonald's, she continually built on her successes. The same can be said for Elon Musk, Warren Buffet, Bill Gates, Michael Jordan, and you!

Just like Cordia Harrington, many successful people have learned to build upon past successes and transfer that success to other areas of life. This ability to leverage past successes and to reach for new ones is called momentum.

The more action you take, the easier it will be to take future action. The more challenges you overcome, the more confident you'll be in overcoming future challenges.

EVERY EXPERIENCE YOU HAVE THAT MOVES YOU FORWARD AND DEMONSTRATES THAT YOU HAVE THE ABILITY TO WORK THROUGH THINGS WILL ENCOURAGE FUTURE SUCCESS.

In some ways, this will become habit naturally as you take repeated action. However, you don't want to leave that to chance. You want to leverage past experience and reach for greater success intentionally. You want to build lifelong momentum.

Narrow focus on only a single goal is the antithesis to building momentum because once it is achieved, there is nothing in place to aspire to. You have a broader focus on who you are becoming, which enables you to see how each achievement builds momentum for the next.

The six core principles of building momentum are your key to setting and achieving greater goals in the future.

They include:

- Avoid Starting Over
- Develop Good Habits
- Establish Action Chains
- Make It Easy to Do
- Pare Down Your Decisions
- Keep Your Purpose Front and Center

CHAPTER 9

Don't Dare to Start Over

"It does not matter how slowly you go as long as you do not stop."

—CONFUCIUS

First, avoid starting over. When an object is at rest, it has something called static friction. This force is difficult to overcome due to "starting resistance." However, once overcome, it is much easier to keep the object in motion.

Some believe that they should stop and take a break when things become difficult. The problem with this is that they risk never starting again. You want to avoid starting over, to keep going no matter how slowly. Because, you know how much easier it is to keep going than it is to start over.

For reference, it takes nearly 7 times as much energy to get a train moving than it does to keep it moving.[16] The same could be said for you.

STARTING FORCES 1.1

How often do you start something, fall off the wagon, and then can't get started again? It is arduous work starting over, and over, and over. The single biggest factor to building momentum is to avoid starting over. Every time you start over, you spend a tremendous amount of energy. And the more often you must start over, the less energy you can direct toward making progress.

Make sure that whatever you're working toward, you do something every single day, no matter how small, to keep you moving toward the goal. Because even small incremental effort will produce more momentum than stalling and struggling to start over.

No matter how insignificant you believe the action is, do it. If you can convince yourself not to do something small and insignificant, how much easier will it be for you to disregard something big?

As a notable example of this, people who weigh themselves every day are more successful at losing weight and keeping it off. The reason is simple, by doing that one small action every day, they avoid starting over.

Even as their eating and exercise change daily, this one simple act is enough to build momentum. Their goal and progress are in front of them daily, encouraging them to take small decisions throughout the day to stay on track.

When you avoid starting over, you force creativity. The fewer choices you have, the more creative you are forced to be.

WHEN YOU ALLOW YOURSELF TO BELIEVE YOU CAN START OVER, YOU DISREGARD ANY VALUE THAT YOU'VE CREATED.

In 1957, two engineers from New Jersey tried to create a new form of wallpaper by placing two shower curtains together, which created air bubbles. Although the fad at the time was highly textured wallpaper, their product never sold.[17]

They didn't scrap their idea and start over though; instead, they turned around and marketed their product as insulation for greenhouses. Again, the product failed to sell. Still they didn't start over. They took what they had and moved forward

Eventually, Alfred Fielding and Marc Chavannes found success using their product to protect items during shipping. Their first big break was when IBM choose to use bubble wrap to ship their computers.

Imagine the difference in results and momentum if Alfred Fielding and Marc Chavannes had started over every time they fell short.

And what about Lamborghini, which originally manufactured tractors. In fact, tractors continue to be manufactured under the Lamborghini brand and logo.

Ferruccio Lamborghini became a master mechanic while serving during World War II. When he completed his service, rather than start over, he bought surplus military machines at a discount. Then, carrying his skills forward, he converted these machines into tractors. Lamborghini became extremely successful building tractors.[18]

He didn't start over when making the switch to producing sports cars. Lamborghini himself admitted that he never invented anything, he simply improved on what was already there. This includes combining the 12-cylinder Ferrari motor with twin cams from the Alpha Romeo. He was a master of not starting over in order to carry his momentum forward.

You are just as capable of not starting over and building on what is already there. You also recognize how slowed progress is more rejuvenating and inspiring than stopping completely.

As you avoid starting over, you will build consistency. This consistency is the number one factor to your momentum. And when you avoid starting over, you are also able to develop good habits.

Quick Tips:

1. *Leverage where you've been into where you're going. Even if you need to shift directions, you should always look for how what you've learned can be leveraged into what you are trying to accomplish.*

When you truly look, there will always be alignments.

2. *Look for the good and shine it. Sometimes when people try to "start over," it's because all they see is the bad and are trying to escape it. When all you see is the bad, it means you haven't spent enough time looking for the good. Look for the good, then polish and shine it so that it overtakes the bad. As you do this, you'll have less desire to start over.*

3. *Slow down to speed up. If you're at a place where you need to slow down, do it but do it with purpose. Slow down in order to plan your next step and then get moving in that direction, slow down to speed up.*

CHAPTER 10

Stop Habits from Killing Your Goals

"Good habits are the key to all success. Bad habits are the unlocked door to failure."

—OG MANDINO

Much of your life is routine, or in other words, habit. A study from Duke University found that as many as 45% of daily decisions are based on habit.[19] If you want to build momentum, you will want to learn the process of developing good habits.

People with a failure attitude focus exclusively on breaking bad habits. Yet, even when those habits are broken, they are rarely replaced with productive ones. You realize the power of breaking bad habits and establishing new productive habits. You get excited about how a new habit can move you toward your goals.

Every habit is a formulation of three things: a trigger, an action, and a reward. In order to change a bad habit and develop a good habit, you must address at least one of those three factors.

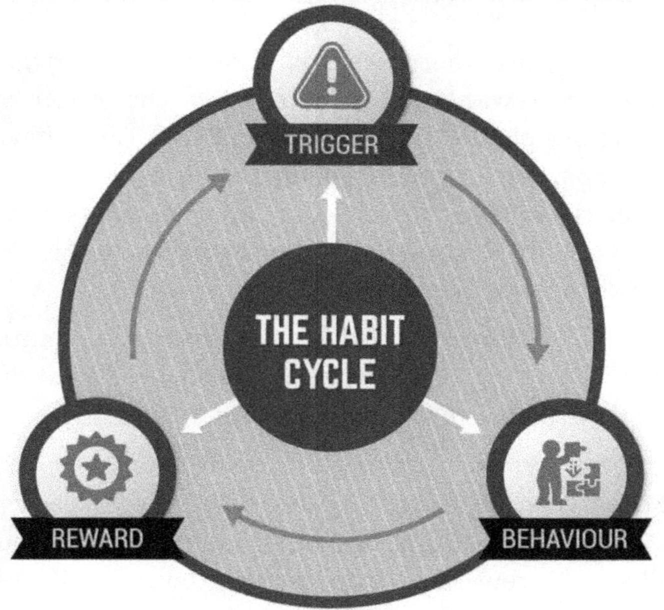

IMAGE 10.1

Take Susan, a proven leader at a large animal health facility who I worked with. She began to utilize *Escalate* in order to launch a new service for exotic species. As she began to implement the process, she struggled to focus on priorities. As we explored her struggle, it came out that at the end of each day, she was so tired from work that she spent no time planning for the next day. She would tell herself to do it in the morning.

However, each morning she would open her phone and instantly see dozens of alerts and emails. Before she knew it, she was caught up in responding to emails and putting out fires. This habit was a tremendous barrier to focusing on priorities; she needed to change it.

Recognizing that the process of habit includes triggers, actions, and rewards, she explored each. The trigger was opening her phone and viewing the alerts. The behavior was jumping right into responding and problem-solving. And the reward was a sense of accomplishment (whether correct or not). She could have chosen to disrupt this cycle at any of these three points.

For example, she could remove the trigger by committing to plan for her day before opening her phone. Rather than seeing her phone in the morning and being triggered to check email, she could turn it into a trigger to plan.

She could change the action by choosing to ignore the alerts and opening a list of priorities first-thing. Or, she could challenge the reward by accepting that "busy" work rarely produces much value.

After considering each step of the habit process, she felt that simply avoiding her phone until she had planned her priorities would be the most powerful. By making this choice, she avoided the trigger and enabled herself to disrupt the routine.

In just two short weeks, she reported that she had made more progress on the service launch than in the previous six weeks and that developing this new habit deserved credit for her progress.

TO AVOID STARTING OVER AND BECOME CONSISTENT, DISRUPT ONE OF THE THREE ELEMENTS OF HABIT: TRIGGER, ACTION, OR REWARD.

Be intentional and personal about your habits. One major pitfall is to over-rely on the habits of others, rather than forming your own. While there is value in learning the habits of successful people, it's important to recognize that those habits work for them. You will be more successful if you customize your own habits, rather than just trying to imitate those of another person.

Be sure to use habits as a means of ridding yourself of bad behaviors and as a means of developing routines that elevate your productivity.

This cycle of habit is an action chain, or a series of actions that lead to an outcome. While disrupting the cycle of habit is powerful, we are not limited to fixing broken action chains (i.e., bad habits), we can establish completely new ones. This is the third way to build momentum, create goal-oriented action chains.

Quick Tips:

1. *Be imperfect. Changing habits can be tough work! Plan for this going into it and allow yourself to be imperfect. Improvement and progress are all that matter, not perfection.*

2. *Add a "but" to your negative thoughts. When you catch yourself in a negative thought pattern like "I can't do this..." insert a "but" and finish the thought. I can't do this but if I keep trying I will be able to.*

3. *Commit to a short timeline. Rather than entering into habit change with a lifelong mentality, try sticking with it for 7 days, 30 days, or 3 months. This will help prevent you from feeling like it is impossible or overwhelming.*

CHAPTER 11

Create Goal-Oriented Action Chains

"Those who do not move, do not notice their chains."

—ROSA LUXEMBURG

An action chain is a series of behaviors intended to produce a result. They tend to be simple and short-term. For example, when you get home, you will hang up that picture you've been meaning to for the last 6 months, is an action chain.

While generally action chains are short-term, they can also be long-term and take the shape of habits. Like, when you get home, you will spend 10 minutes talking to your family about their day. Habits are a form of action chains, but here the focus is on short-term action chains to accomplish a specific task.

An additional distinction is that habits are more meaningful for long-term repetitive behaviors, whereas action chains can be used for short-term, necessary ones and for long-term ones.

THE GREATEST VALUE OF ACTION CHAINS IS IN TAKING UNINTENTIONAL WASTED TIME AND TURNING IT INTO PRODUCTIVITY.

Too many in the world believe they should get credit for good intentions. They wonder why, with all their good intention, they aren't achieving their goals. You realize that if you want to achieve your goals, you must turn good intentions into action through goal-oriented action chains.

To build a new action chain, start by creating a "When, Then" commitment. In this way, you can add new actions to daily experiences. For example, rather than committing "I will spend 5 minutes working on my goal," create an action chain by committing, "When I finish my lunch, I will immediately spend 5 minutes working on my goal."

Rather than being an isolated action, it is now part of an action chain—and research has shown that these action chains are more powerful than isolated commitments.[20]

As with long-term habits, it is beneficial to add a reward to your action chain. While progress itself is a reward, if you are just starting to build lifelong momentum, build into the action chain a desirable reward.

One thing that you have already learned is how challenging it is to achieve ambiguous goals. Likewise, it is difficult to execute ambiguous action chains. Unfortunately, that's often how you've done it in the past.

Instead of a clear and definable action chain, you tell yourself things like, "I'll do it tomorrow" or "When I have the energy, then I'll do it." These things are unclear, so even if it does happen, it's unclear when and how the next action will be triggered. Tomorrow comes, and you go on with your day because you weren't clear about when. You have the energy, but you weren't clear about how to remember your action chain.

Ambiguous action chains are one thing, but evasive ones are another. An evasive action chain is feigned intention. It is when you place one task in front of a better task as a form of procrastination because the better activity is not one you want to do. Have you ever caught yourself creating an evasive action chain? Maybe you say, "When I finish repairing the fence, I'll do it"—knowing full well that you will turn repairing the fence into an all-day job.

A large ranching operation I consulted with found evasive action chains were so prevalent that it cost their organization nearly $25,000 a year. How? Employees would receive a job duty, such as repairing a fence. Then, inevitably a couple of hours into the project they would determine that they needed different materials to complete the job. Getting those materials would require them to "run into town."

Most of the time, the trip to town was unnecessary; they could have completed the job with the materials they had on hand. Going to town was an evasive choice, and the evasive action chain was in motion. While at the hardware store, they would decide to buy excessive materials to prevent future unnecessary trips to town. Yet, those excessive materials were thrown into a barn and forgotten about.

When we organized and took inventory of the disordered barns, we found over $1,500 in duct tape alone. These trips to town added up in terms of fuel, employee time, and unnecessary materials. The original choice seemed innocuous enough, but it's the action chain that it set into motion that was costly. For them, the cost was nearly $25,000 annually. How much are your evasive action chains costing you?

When you work to build goal-oriented action chains, focus your attention on your goal and be specific with your "When, Then" statements.

As you develop productive action chains, you will look for a balance between creating the right behaviors and limiting the wrong ones. Too often individuals invest so much time and effort into preventing the wrong behaviors that they lack the energy to perform the right ones.

The traditional focus on creating barriers to the wrong behaviors (e.g., we lock away the junk food and restrict access to time-wasters), doesn't ensure that good ones will take their place. By reprogramming your habits and creating action chains, you encourage new productive behaviors to replace the old destructive ones.

With action chains in your repertoire, you will quickly turn good intentions into meaningful actions.

Quick Tips:

1. *Define the target. Rather than starting at the very beginning and forcing an action into your day, start with the end in mind. Define what the target action is, then ask yourself, where can I most naturally*

insert this action into my day? This will make it much easier to carry out.

2. *Reinforce the nearest approximations. Just like new habits, you won't always be successful the first time when creating a new action chain. In order to encourage repetition, you should reinforce and reward the nearest approximations. Maybe you didn't spend 30 minutes on it like you planned out, but if you started on it and that was more than before, then this is the nearest approximation, and you should reinforce it through reward.*

3. *Monitor results. Pay attention to your results, specifically how you feel when you carry out the goal-oriented action chain versus when you don't. By forcing yourself to acknowledge how successful efforts and unsuccessful efforts make you feel, you won't be able to ignore them as easily. The next time your cue comes up to start the action chain, you'll remember this reflection and will be more likely to follow through.*

CHAPTER 12

Make it Easy to Do

"The path of least resistance is the path of most allowance."

– ABRAHAM

Don't be like your friends who are focused on putting up endless barriers to the things they want to avoid. You're too good at removing barriers for that to work. Instead, you want to be the person who enables yourself to succeed at the right things.

You are wired to take the path of least resistance. Just like water or any other physical element. So much so that researchers Nobuhiro Hagura, Patrick Haggard, and Jorn Diedrichsen found that even slight resistance to the right choice over the wrong choice created bias toward the wrong choice.[21]

They asked volunteers to move one of two levers. While looking at a screen with dots, the volunteers were asked to move the right-hand lever if the dots were moving to the right or the left-hand lever if they were moving to the left.

What the volunteers didn't know was that the researchers added a small amount of resistance to one of the levers. This slight resistance changed the action of the volunteers. When resistance was on the left lever, they showed a preference for the right lever and vice versa. Even when the motion of the dots was in conflict.

This research shows something many of you know all too well, you will do what's easy to do.

You intuitively know this, it's why you make the things you don't want to do, difficult to do. You create barriers to things you want to stop doing. Maybe you remove junk food from the house, go out of your way to avoid a difficult colleague, or have restrictions for social media.

While putting barriers in place to prevent undesirable actions has its own merit, it does not ensure that the right things get done. It only helps prevent the wrong things from getting done.

This is when you want to make it easy to do. Rather than focusing on how you can prevent bad behaviors, focus on how you can make the good behaviors easy to do. You will love the power of this simple change. It will catalyze your action chains and habit formation. Ask yourself, "How can I make this good behavior easy to do?"

Disney understands how making things easy to do can transform behavior. The story goes that after buying a hot dog one day, Walt Disney walked about thirty feet before finishing it. He turned and said, "There needs to be a trash can here." Today trash cans are strategically placed every thirty feet around Disney parks.

This practice of making things easy to do has spread as well. Philadelphia City Council passed a plan in 2015 requiring all food establishments to have trash and recycle bins outside their storefronts.[22]

When you make things easy to do, they are more likely to get done.

In 2007, I was running an international freight brokerage with a high amount of outside sales. This meant that employees made dozens of cold calls every day. However, I found that barely half the target of fifty calls was being made.

In observing actions each morning, I discovered that several employees procrastinated make calls by justifying low-value emails and performing client research. My first instinct was to create barriers to these things before 9:30 a.m., in hopes that they would make cold calls during that time. This didn't help, and they just found new ways to procrastinate.

After discussing the problem with employees, they brought up several perceived challenges, like not knowing exactly who to call or what to say. So, we began creating specific lists for employees to call and giving them a script.

Instead of asking them to make cold calls, I made it easy to do by giving them everything they needed including a simple script. If they made the call and followed the script, it was considered a success.

It wasn't until I took this step, to make the right behavior easy to do, that it actually started getting done.

Whatever your solutions, they can be very simple. Maybe it is to lay out all the necessary materials beforehand, schedule an energizing playlist to start at a specific time, or let others know you need the space at a set time.

Anything you do to make the good behavior easy to do will make it more likely to happen.

SPEND AS MUCH TIME MAKING THE RIGHT THINGS EASY TO DO, AS YOU DO MAKING THE WRONG THINGS HARD.

A theme you may have noticed throughout is the importance of encouraging the right things to happen, rather than investing energy in preventing the wrong things. The world will tell you to invest your energy in preventing bad things, but goals can only be achieved by doing the right things.

One consideration in this process is to eliminate distracting decisions. Read on to learn about paring down your decisions.

Quick Tips:

1. *Plan better. The most obvious way that you can make it easy to do is to plan better. Whatever it is that you intend to do, think through all the things that you will need in order to do it successfully. Get those materials and resources in place long before you need them so that when you need to follow through, you'll be able to do it effectively.*

2. *Be prepared. Planning is about getting all the right resources in place, and preparing is about*

anticipating the unexpected. Consider what could distract or prevent you from following through, then prepare for how you will deal with those distractions and barriers beforehand. If you're prepared beforehand, the impact will be far less than if you're trying to adjust in the moment.

3. *Ask for help. One way to make it easy is to ask for someone's help. Even small amounts of help will distribute some of the burden off of you, making your lift lighter and ultimately making the task easier to do. Think small at first, can you ask for a reminder? Can you ask for advice? Ask for help in small ways.*

CHAPTER 13

Pare Down Your Decisions

"Making a true decision means committing to achieving a result, and then cutting yourself off from any other possibility."

– TONY ROBBINS

One quick way to make the right things easy to do is to pare down your decisions. You make up to 35,000 decisions per day, and every conscious decision you make requires intellectual bandwidth.

The majority of people are accustomed to saying "yes" to everything. They spread themselves thin and find that they can't do it all. You are different. You are good at saying "no" to some things, so that you can say "yes" to the right things.

The more decisions you have to make, the less energy you can place on each decision. In fact, there is a term for being overwhelmed by decision-making; no surprise, psychologists refer to this as "decision fatigue." It occurs when you spend so much mental energy making choices that you lose the ability to focus on key details.

I experienced this limited bandwidth early in my consulting career. My mentor was constantly giving me great advice about how to better facilitate a room full of executives. I wanted desperately to be able to facilitate like the seasoned veteran that he was, so I tried to incorporate every insight into my facilitation.

However, I found when I got into the room, that I was trying to do too many things. And, by trying to implement every great idea he shared, I was doing a poor job across the board. My energy was spread too thin across many decisions.

During our next conversation, I asked my mentor, "What are the top three things you focus on while facilitating a group of executives?" He replied, "I focus on the purpose for having the meeting, the attitudes among participants, and simplifying their choices in practical terms."

In that instant, my laundry list of actions in the room was pared down to three simple things. The next time I stepped into the room, I wrote those three things at the top of my notebook and constantly looked at them throughout the session. It was by far the best facilitation I had ever performed.

By paring down my own decisions, I was able to free up bandwidth and energy to focus on the most valuable tasks.

YOU TOO CAN ALLEVIATE DECISION FATIGUE AND FOCUS ON HIGH PRIORITY ACTIONS BY PARING DOWN DECISIONS. YOU DO THIS BY CUTTING THE DECISION ASPECT OF SIMPLE AND MUNDANE CHOICES.

Mark Zuckerberg famously pares down his decisions by wearing the same shirt every day. And, he's not alone. Former President Barack Obama and the late Steve Jobs also wore the same outfits every day to avoid wasting time and mental energy on these mundane decisions.

Another example includes British millionaire entrepreneur and investor Peter Jones, he pares down his decisions by eating the same thing every morning for breakfast. What simple and mundane decisions are you wasting time on?

One of the best ways to pare down decisions is to defer them to others, delegate. Many times, when asked by my spouse or team to decide, I will reply with, "I don't have the bandwidth to make that decision, please make it for us." However, the rule is that if I've invited support to pare down my decisions, I cannot later complain about those decisions.

The added benefit to inviting others to make decisions is that you avoid getting distracted. Research shows that it takes an average of 23 minutes and 15 seconds to get back to the previous task after getting distracted.[23] By quickly delegating decisions, you avoid this recovery time. Even two quickly delegated decisions can gain you 45 minutes of productivity.

Some individuals you know feel the need to be involved in every decision, but this micro-managing style is destructive, especially when it comes to accomplishing goals. You care more about achieving your goals than you do managing every decision yourself.

As you pare down decisions, you can make sure they are the right ones by keeping your purpose front and center. Be careful to not drop decisions that actually give you energy versus rob you of energy.

Quick Tips:

1. *Identify what you'll sacrifice. Some paring of decisions requires sacrifice. Before you start cutting off random decisions, clearly define what you are willing to sacrifice. Then start with the most minimal sacrifice and work your way up over time as needed.*
2. *Remove what you don't like. You can start to pare decisions by looking for daily decisions that you don't like making. Then ask which of those actually matter, specifically with your goal in mind. One friend I worked with used this method to eliminate cooking—she simply cooked all of her meals on one day, so that she didn't have to make the decision all the other days.*
3. *Use goal-oriented action chains to prevent a decision. Action chains can be used to stop an action, just like they can be used to start one. Once you've identified a decision you want to let go of, build a goal-oriented action chain that redirects that decision by articulating what you won't do, rather than what you will.*

CHAPTER 14

Keep Your Purpose Front and Center

"It's not enough to have lived. We should be determined to live for something."

– WINSTON S. CHURCHILL

The final and possibly most important principle of building moment is to keep your purpose front and center. If you trace your choices back, they will always lead you to purpose. Sometimes this can be a difficult reality to accept because it reveals truths you may not want to accept.

The reason is that you can't claim your purpose is one thing, if your actions contradict it. Your actions will lead you back to purpose, whether you like the place they lead you back to or not.

Many of those who have stalled on their goals are trying to solve them intellectually. The problem is that data, facts, and figures do not mobilize people. You appreciate the power of emotion to mobilize you, therefore you use purpose to engage the power of emotion.

You've heard it time and time again, you need a clear and compelling vision of why you want to accomplish your goal. The reason? Purpose is what gives you the energy to keep moving forward and building momentum. If you don't have a compelling purpose, the moment things get challenging, you may give up on your goal.

When too much focus is placed on the intellectual factors of success, the crucial aspects of emotion are ignored. While good ideas can help build the map, emotion will get you moving. In fact, the word emotion comes from Latin and French, referring to "in motion." *E*motion is what sets you *in* motion.

Purpose is how you engage the energy from emotion in your goals, it is the deep-seated drive that will keep you going. Whenever you find yourself bogged down in difficult tasks, take a moment to put them into perspective. Bring your purpose front and center to remember why you care about this goal. While you may not enjoy the task at hand, it will be much easier to complete when you make the connection to purpose.

Muhammad Ali epitomized this when he said, "I hated every minute of training, but I said, 'Don't quit. Suffer now and live the rest of your life as a champion.'" This purpose gave him the energy to push through a grueling training schedule. A friend of mine who was on her own grueling fitness journey would tell herself, "Nothing tastes as good as it feels to be fit" in order to keep her purpose front and center.

As Muhammad Ali demonstrated, the first way to keep purpose front and center is to place each decision you make into the broader context of your purpose. Doing this is what enables individuals to make extreme sacrifices in the name of a goal—they place each decision into the context of that goal.

By placing each decision into the broader context of your purpose, they will begin to add up to something bigger than they would individually.

In the compelling article *Change or Die*, Alan Deutschman highlights how survivors of coronary artery bypass surgery don't change their behavior for data and statistics. According to Dr. Edward Miller, 90% of these survivors haven't changed their lifestyle two years after coronary-artery bypass grafting—even after receiving all of the statistics.[24]

However, when health care professionals and patients connect lifestyle changes to broader purposes and goals, such as spending more active time with loved ones, 77% will stick with these lifestyle changes.

The power of purpose to compel you toward your goals should not be underestimated.

Another way to keep purpose front and center is to let it take the lead. Far too often, we let our schedules, routines, and mundane tasks take the lead, which leaves little room for purpose. The late Stephen R. Covey advised: "Don't prioritize your schedule, schedule your priorities."

Rather than simply looking at all the tasks that are on your schedule and rushing through them aimlessly, start with your purpose, whether they are already on your calendar or not, and build your schedule from that purpose.

Whatever your chosen method, you want to find a way to keep your purpose front and center, if you don't, you risk losing sight of what matters and procrastinating the most important tasks. The passion you find when you keep your purpose front and center will energize you to push forward.

As you use the six principles of momentum; 1) Avoid Starting Over, 2) Develop Good Habits, 3) Establish Action Chains, 4) Make It Easy To Do, 5) Pare Down Your Decisions, and 6) Keep Your Purpose Front and Center, you will build momentum. And, as this happens, your aspirations, goals, and achievements will grow exponentially.

Quick Tips:

1. *Make it personal. If you articulate your purpose in a way that isn't personal, not only will it be harder to remember, it will be less likely to stick. Make it personal by stating it in a way that only means something to you. Have a movie you love? Use a line or character from the movie to help you remember (example: to be the Bagger Vance of strategy☺)*

2. *Wear a reminder. Use a token that is with you regularly to remind you, maybe it's a necklace, bracelet, or coin like Cordia. Studies actually show*

that the more random the object, the more likely it is to be effective.

3. *Ask "Why?" a lot! Because life is happening all around you, it can be easy to just scratch the surface of reason. By asking yourself and others "Why?" you start to dig below the surface and get closer to purpose. This simple question is possibly the most important question you can ask and will automatically start to focus attention on more purpose-oriented ideas. Alternatively, you can ask, "What's the purpose?"*

WHAT'S NEXT?

You have the tool you need to achieve your goals because action is that tool. You have learned the principles of taking action and building momentum and are now prepared to immediately progress toward those goals.

The only way to achieve your goals is to actually use the tool, to take action. And when the action you take doesn't move you toward your goal, you must choose a more powerful action.

You can spend all the time, money, and energy you want building desire, but ultimately Action + Desire = Progress. You can also continue to spin your wheels trying the same thing over and over again. Don't! If what you've tried hasn't worked, don't back away from it, don't choose something smaller, *Escalate* and choose a more powerful way of getting things done.

Your goals are just a few actions away from being reality, you know it and can feel it. What you need though are the right actions. The remainder of *Escalate* will show you which actions to take and how to choose more powerful actions when you're not making the progress you want.

If you're just getting started and have struggled for a long time to achieve a meaningful goal, you may want to start with the *ActionHacks* and the core principle of *Escalate*, which is to continuously choose a more powerful approach to achieving your goal. This alone is often enough to overcome "starting resistance."

However, when you're truly stuck and have built habits that are keeping you from moving, follow the step-by-step *Escalate Process* as outlined next. If you commit to following the practice as outlined, you will get unstuck and build momentum!

Learn the full step-by-step *Escalate Process* next.

SECTION 2: THE ESCALATE PROCESS

The Step-by-Step Process for Getting Unstuck and Building Momentum

Now that you know the core action and momentum principles of...

A. Action + Desire = Progress

B. Action Perpetuates Action

C. Progress Inspires Greater Progress

D. Extraordinary is a Result, Not an Action

E. Failure is Evidence of Greater Potential

F. Avoid Starting Over

G. Develop Good Habits

H. Establish Goal-Oriented Action Chains

I. Make It Easy To Do

J. Pare Down Your Decisions

K. Keep Your Purpose and Priorities Front and Center

You need a straightforward process to get yourself unstuck and build lifelong momentum. The *Escalate Process* provides a step-by-step way to do exactly that.

The original process of *Escalate* was developed to help corporate and small business clients get out of a rut with projects. And to help them choose more powerful ways of accomplishing tasks, rather than weaker ways. As with any goal, hurdles and challenges were faced. Action was taken to address any flaws in the process and fine-tune the method to arrive at the process shared with you today.

Escalate is a process that anyone can apply and follow. To get an immediate start, you can refer to the *ActionHacks* at the end of the book. However, for the most potent results, read and learn the entire process before implementing it.

So what is the *Escalate Process*?

The *Escalate Process* outlined here is specifically designed to get you unstuck and to build lifelong momentum. It doesn't matter what your goal is, if you follow the *Escalate Process* you will get unstuck and build momentum. If you've read Section One of this book, you will recognize how those learnings are applied simply and practically through the *Escalate Process*.

There is a major point that needs to be made now. The *Escalate Process* is not a cure-all for life, it is a method designed to ensure you achieve your very specific goal. For general life principles of desire and action refer back to Section One.

While there are components of the *Escalate Process* that you will find broad application for, keep in mind that this process has one intent in mind, and that is to ensure you achieve a specific goal by getting unstuck and building momentum. The *Escalate Process* is very rigid in this intent.

Here is the process:

Step #1: Map out the tasks you must complete to achieve your goal through unpacking, ordering, and prioritizing.

Step #2: Choose a task and a method (referred to as escalations) to accomplish it.

Step #3a: If you complete the task successfully, recognize your progress and reward yourself. Then, move on to the next task based on order and priority.

Step #3b: If you did not complete the task successfully, pay for it, then *Escalate* it by choosing a more powerful method of accomplishing the task.

Step #4: Repeat Step #2 and Step #3 until you either accomplish the task or need to *Escalate* a task three times. Once you have Escalated a task three times, immediately outsource that task.

Step #5: Prune unnecessary tasks by removing them, moving on to the next task, and testing the impact of not completing the prior one.

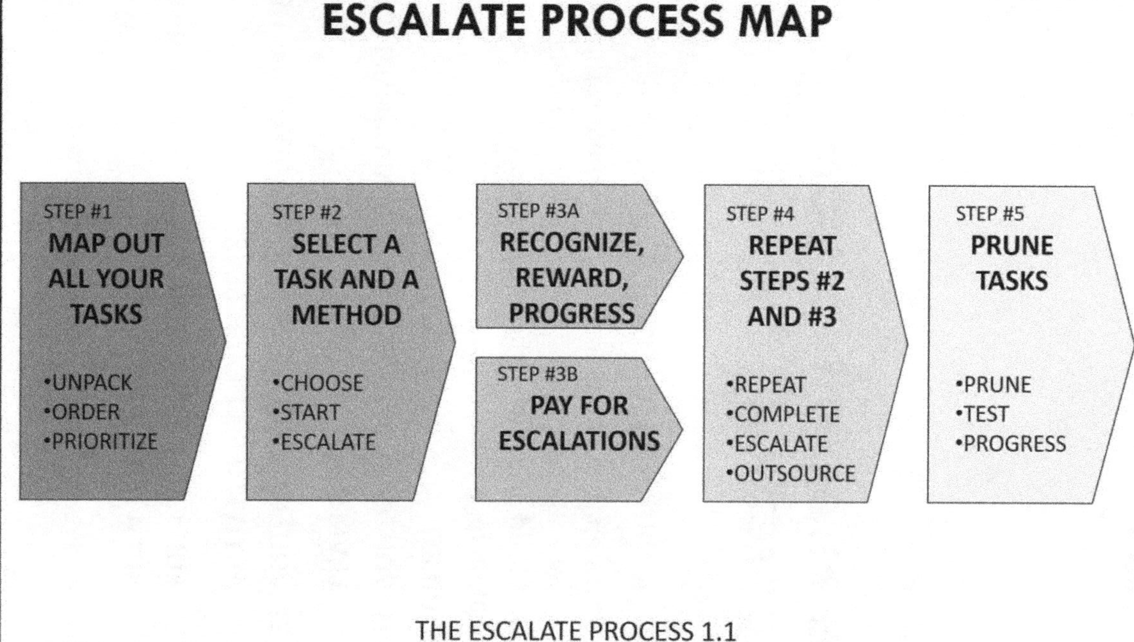

THE ESCALATE PROCESS 1.1

STEP #1: DRAFT YOUR GOAL PROGRESSION

UNPACK, ORDER, PRIORITIZE

The first step in the Escalate Process is about setting your foundation. By unpacking your goal, ordering your activities, and prioritizing the highest value work, you set a foundation for success.

THE RULES:

1) **YOU CAN ONLY UNPACK A MAXIMUM OF 3 LEVELS**
2) **YOU CAN ONLY ORDER A MAXIMUM OF 3 ACTIVITIES AT EACH LEVEL**
3) **YOU CAN ONLY PRIORITIZE A MAXIMUM OF 3 ACTIVITIES AT A TIME**

There are three practices to embrace in Step #1:

The first is Unpack. As previously mentioned, this is a method to chunk (or break down) large goals into smaller more task-based activities.

The second practice is to Order. This is a method to identify which activities must be performed first to enable other activities to be completed.

The third practice is to Prioritize. This is a method to focus your attention on the highest value activities.

As has been covered, sometimes the obstacle keeping you from moving forward is being overwhelmed with the task at hand—a result of setting a sizeable goal and wondering how you will ever achieve it.

ESTABLISHING S.M.A.R.T. GOALS

S.M.A.R.T. goals are Specific, Measurable, Achievable, Relevant, and Time-bound.

Specific requires us to answer the who, what, when, where, and why questions. I will decrease the hiring process by 2 weeks by automating the screening process by the end of the year to reduce the number of applicants that we lose to other companies.

Measurable refers to the way we define progress. We cannot measure diligence, but we can measure and benchmark how often we get sidetracked or the time it takes us to accomplish a task.

Achievable simply forces us to consider whether the goal is realistic. This requires us to consider the "How?" question and past performance. Doubling sales could be a long shot if we have been way below quotas in the past and need planning but could be uninspiring if sales have been tripling for the last quarter.

Relevant states that the goal must be important to you. If it isn't worthwhile or aligned with your other goals, you will not have the purpose or bandwidth for the undertaking. Losing weight and learning how to bake cakes may not be the most complementary endeavors.

Time-bound forces you to create a deadline for the goal. It is beneficial to create mini-deadlines to evaluate effort and adjust. I will increase my income by $1000 per month by the end of the year and will make a specific number of calls every week.

Unpack

To move past feeling overwhelmed, you want to unpack your big goal into smaller more manageable tasks. This process is only useful if you identify what the exact activity is that you are to perform.

If you unpack your big goal into tasks that are unclear or ambiguous, it will not help you move forward. If this happens, you should return to your goal and rethink how you unpack each level to ensure you arrive at clear and specific tasks.

By unpacking your goal, you draft out a plan of progression. In this way, you don't have to guess at whether you're progressing or not, you can visibly see as you achieve small goals and move closer to accomplishing your big goal.

Additionally, unpacking your big goal intentionally ensures the actions you take are connected to your goal, rather than random or unrelated. Without unpacking, you can find yourself doing things that you feel are valuable but are actually unrelated to your goal and are in reality just busywork.

Start the process of unpacking by listing every activity that you believe it will take to accomplish your goal. We'll use Alexander's story as an example throughout the *Escalate Process*.

Alexander is a 33-year-old aspiring entrepreneur. He has been working as an account manager for a telecom company for six years, but his dream is to start a side business producing customized apparel and selling it through boutique shops and online.

His big goal is to make an additional $75,000 a year through this business working less than 15 hours per week, within the next 18 months. However, Alexander has had this dream for nearly three years and isn't any closer to achieving it today than when he first dreamed it.

Using the *Escalate Process*, Alexander starts to unpack his overwhelming goal by writing out every task he can think of that it will take to achieve it.

We won't list all of the activities here, but some of the steps necessary to achieve his goal include choosing a business name, forming a business entity, designing the pieces, finding a manufacturer, researching materials, researching payment processing, selecting payment processing, testing designs, building a website, creating social media accounts, and creating a marketing strategy.

As you brainstorm all of the tasks it will take to achieve your goal, some of them will be bigger than others. The bigger tasks will be your first unpacked level, because they will require you to unpack them even further.

At this stage you have a S.M.A.R.T. goal and your first level of unpacked tasks, looking something like image *Unpack 1.1*.

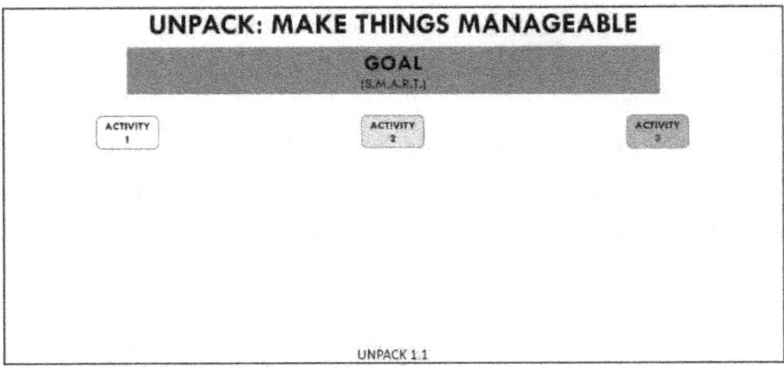

A lot of work goes into getting a piece of apparel to market, and it needs to appeal to the right people. It needs to fit a fad or trend and people need to know it exists. The tasks mentioned above are a start to mapping out how he can achieve this goal. However, each of those activities can be further unpacked.

For example, maybe you don't have the slightest clue about manufacturing apparel. You know that people often do it overseas, but how do you find those manufacturers and establish a relationship with them? How do you choose the materials, negotiate costs, etc.?

For the activities that still feel too big, you want to unpack another level. In this case, take the "find a manufacturer" task and ask, "What will it take to find a manufacturer?"

Some of the next level of tasks for this include online research about how apparel can be manufactured, research about companies that manufacture apparel, reaching out to and connecting with others who have done it, etc. With this even more detailed breakdown you start to get clarity about the path ahead.

What had felt like a colossal task, is now broken down into more manageable activities. You will realize that other activities are still beyond your skill set, so you have to unpack another level for those as well.

As you continue to unpack tasks into their smaller components, you will end up with something that looks like image *Unpack 1.2* with multiple layers of tasks.

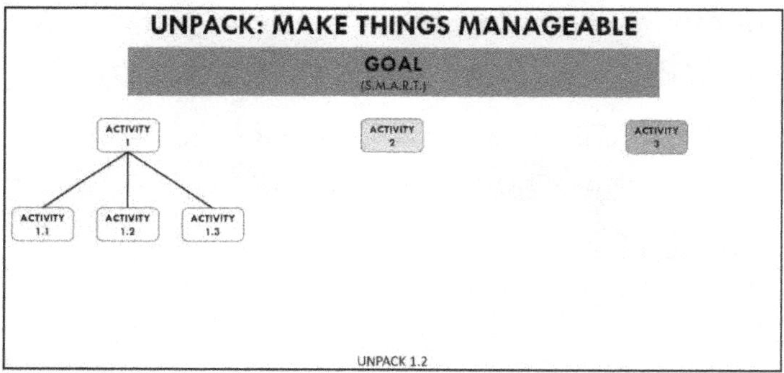

UNPACK 1.2

For creating a business entity, you unpack the following activities:

- Choose a name for your entity
- Research how business entities are formed
- Speak to an attorney and an accountant about different entity types

- Officially form the business entity

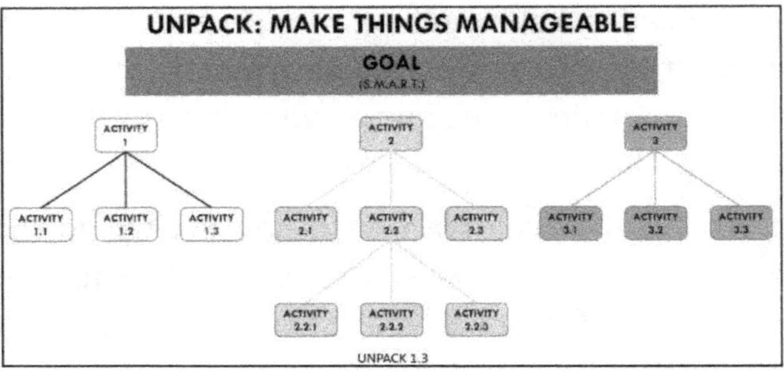

UNPACK 1.3

As you unpack activities, your path ahead will become clearer—rather than overwhelming. The challenge you will run into as you begin to unpack a massive goal is that there are potentially hundreds of activities! The sheer number of tasks can make you feel overwhelmed as you can see in image *Unpack 1.4*.

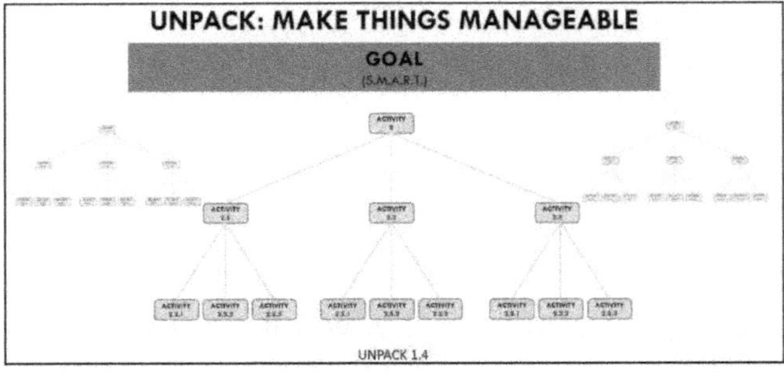

UNPACK 1.4

When this happens, enlist Rule #1: You can only unpack a maximum of three layers of tasks.

Your stated goal does not count as a layer of activity. You have reached the maximum number of layers for unpacking your activity when you have a chain of three interdependent tasks.

For Alexander, his first layer of tasks included finding a manufacturer. When he broke this task down into smaller tasks, one of those was to "reach out to and connect with others who have done it." He could then break this task down even further into identifying others who have done it, drafting an email message to them, sending the email and following up with a call.

He now has three layers. The first layer being "find a manufacturer," the second layer including "reach out to and connect with others who have done it," and the third layer including "identify others who have done it."

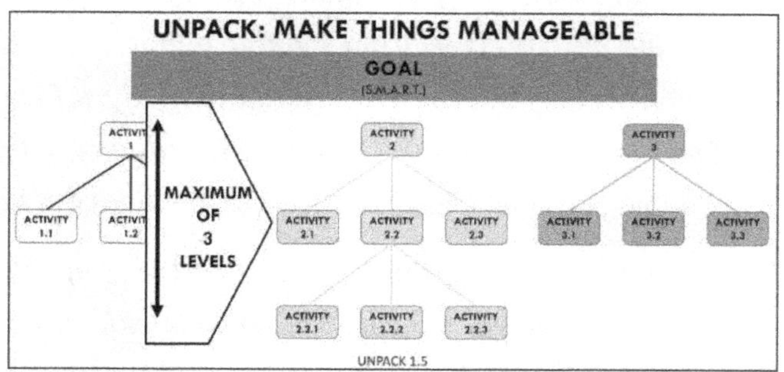

UNPACK 1.5

So why just three layers? You can become overwhelmed by both the size of the task or the number of tasks. This rule exists so that you don't swing to the other side of the spectrum and become overwhelmed by how many tasks you have to do. When you become overwhelmed by either the scale of the task or the number of tasks, the result is the same—you take no action.

If you cannot capture all of the appropriate tasks in three layers, you may be breaking them down too small. The key to unpacking effectively is finding the balance between identifying small enough tasks to feel confident moving forward while keeping them big enough to be meaningful. Tasks that become too small can be easily dismissed.

To keep to three layers, you may need to prioritize your large brainstormed list of tasks while unpacking them. We will cover prioritizing a little later.

Why it works:

a. *Refer to Chapter 7: Be Undaunted from the Start. Unpacking works by making your big goal manageable through small and simple activities. Through unpacking, you identify small goals that are doable, and this is exciting, making it more likely that you will carry out the activity. Additionally, it focuses your energy on the small and simple ordinary actions that will cumulatively produce extraordinary results.*

b. *Refer to Chapter 1: Motivation is a Lie! Unpacking gets you started right away. By unpacking, you've already turned ideas into action. You've now added action to your desire and are making progress!*

To unpack your own goal and set in motion the power of Escalate, download the *Escalate Process* Template in the full online course at kylebrost.com/escalate

Order

Next, you need to order the tasks you've unpacked. Ordering your tasks is about deciding what must come first.

This is different than prioritizing, which is identifying what is most important to achieving your goal.

Ordering helps you to take an extensive list of activities and narrow your focus at the start by forcing you to identify what needs to be completed first in order to complete another task.

Start at the lowest level of tasks and work upwards, considering each one. Ask yourself, "Which of these tasks can be done independently and which of these tasks must wait for another to be completed?" You can work from there with the end goal of tackling three tasks at a time.

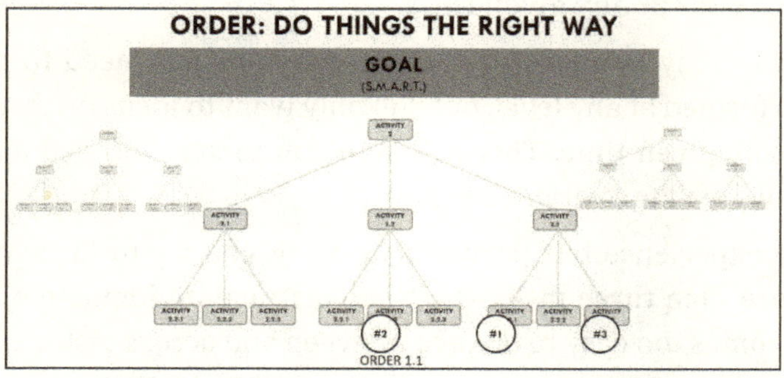

ORDER 1.1

For Alexander, the lowest level of activities includes identifying who has found a manufacturer before, drafting an email message, and sending an email and follow-up call. You have to consider which of these activities can be carried out independently and which cannot be completed until another task has been completed.

If you want to email and call people, you need to know who they are. Therefore, identifying who has done it before, must come first. You decide your first group of activities should follow this order:

1) Create a target list of who has done it before
2) Draft messages to these individuals
3) Reach out to these individuals via email and phone

You may order both within each unpacked layer and across unpacked layers because often the activities that need to happen first are not within a specific, unpacked layer. Activities at any tier or unpacked group may rely on another layer or group. Identify the three activities to start with that aren't dependent on any others.

The rule is that you can only order a maximum of three activities at any given time.

There may be more than three activities that need to be performed at any level, but you only want to focus on three at any given time. This will help you to stay focused and avoid feeling overwhelmed.

My experience has proved that when you try to focus on more than three tasks at a time, distraction dominates. It becomes too easy to bounce between and across tasks, and the recovery time ends up killing your productivity.

Your aim is to break a massive goal into a series of clear and manageable tasks, so you will not feel besieged by the number of activities. The idea is that after you unpack three layers with a MAXIMUM of 39 activities, you can order the first three activities you wish to tackle.

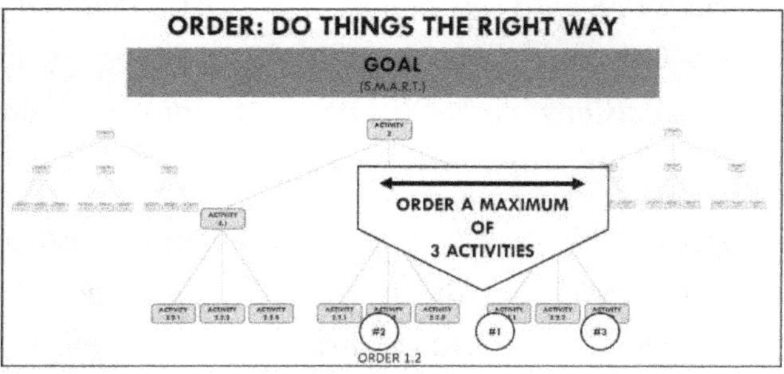

By taking the time to order your activities, you are able to see which tasks can be performed independently and which are dependent on another task. It may seem like a simple way to start, but it is easy to start on an activity with the best of intentions, only to find out that you should have started somewhere else.

After unpacking your goal, order the tasks to make progress more efficiently and avoid costly mistakes that can get you stuck.

Why it works:

a. *Refer to Chapter 9: Don't Dare to Start Over. Ordering prevents you from getting stuck by putting what needs to come first, first. Many people begin at the wrong place and find that they must go back to make progress. When this happens, you become defeated and risk getting stuck. By ordering from the start, you mitigate this risk and avoid having to start over.*

b. *Refer to Chapter 13: Pare Down Your Decisions. Ordering pares down your decisions. Rather than choosing between hundreds of tasks, your choices are narrowed down to a select few, this paring down of decisions makes it easier to direct attention toward the right ones.*

c. *Refer to Chapter 3: Take Action Today to Ensure You Act Tomorrow. By starting on an action today through the order process, you enlist the perpetuating effect of action. Even when it is simply a necessary activity that may not in and of itself be exciting, this action will create future action.*

Prioritize

You now want to prioritize.

Look at all the tasks you've listed and ask yourself, "Which of these activities create the most value?"

First, star them, so you have them marked, then number them in order of priority: #1 being the most valuable, #2 the next most valuable, and so on.

As you look across Alexander's matrix of activities, one surfaces immediately as being the most valuable; it is designing the apparel. This is the priority because that task will dictate his ability to sell a product and connect with customers. The designs hold the most independent value.

However, just because it is the most valuable, does not mean it must come first. For example, identifying others who have done it before could still come before designing.

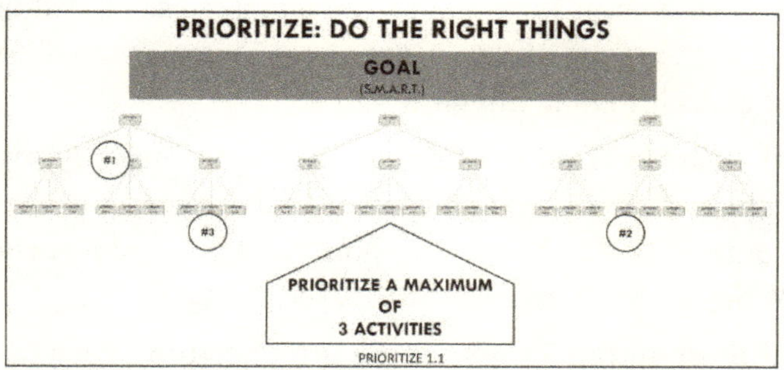

PRIORITIZE 1.1

You may prioritize any number of activities. However, you can only have your top three priorities written on your action plan at any given time. **This is the third rule: you can only focus on 3 Priorities at a time.**

Ok, so now you've unpacked, ordered, and prioritized. You are feeling pretty good about what activities need to be done right now to accomplish your goal.

Where and how do you start?

The simple answer is that you choose one of the activities that you've identified and take a shot at completing it. At this point, you may have anywhere from three activities to 39 activities that need to be completed. You start by choosing the highest priority activity that needs to be done first in order.

Use the Priority Matrix shown in image *PRIORITIZE 1.2* to identify the priority and order of your tasks. With the Priority Matrix, you list all of the tasks you've unpacked. Then you rate each of those tasks on how much independent value the task offers and how directly it is related to your goal. Use a scale of 1-7, where one is low and 7 is high.

You can then plot each task on the matrix to see if it should come first, second, third, or not at all. This matrix will sort your tasks into four categories.

Goal Priority Tasks: These are your top priority tasks, they have high independent value and are directly related to your goal. You should focus on these 1st if you can, and 80% of your effort should be focused here.

Goal Supporting Tasks: These are your top order tasks, they are directly related to your goal, but may have low independent value. They should be focused on 2nd unless a Goal Priority Task is dependent on their completion.

Value-Add Tasks: These are tasks with high independent value but are not directly related to your goal. These should be performed third. You should focus on these tasks in order to improve the quality of your outcomes, but they will not dictate your outcomes...they are truly value-add.

Busywork Tasks: These are tasks that have low independent value and are not directly related to your goal. You should get rid of these tasks as they will not add value, nor will they help you progress toward your goal.

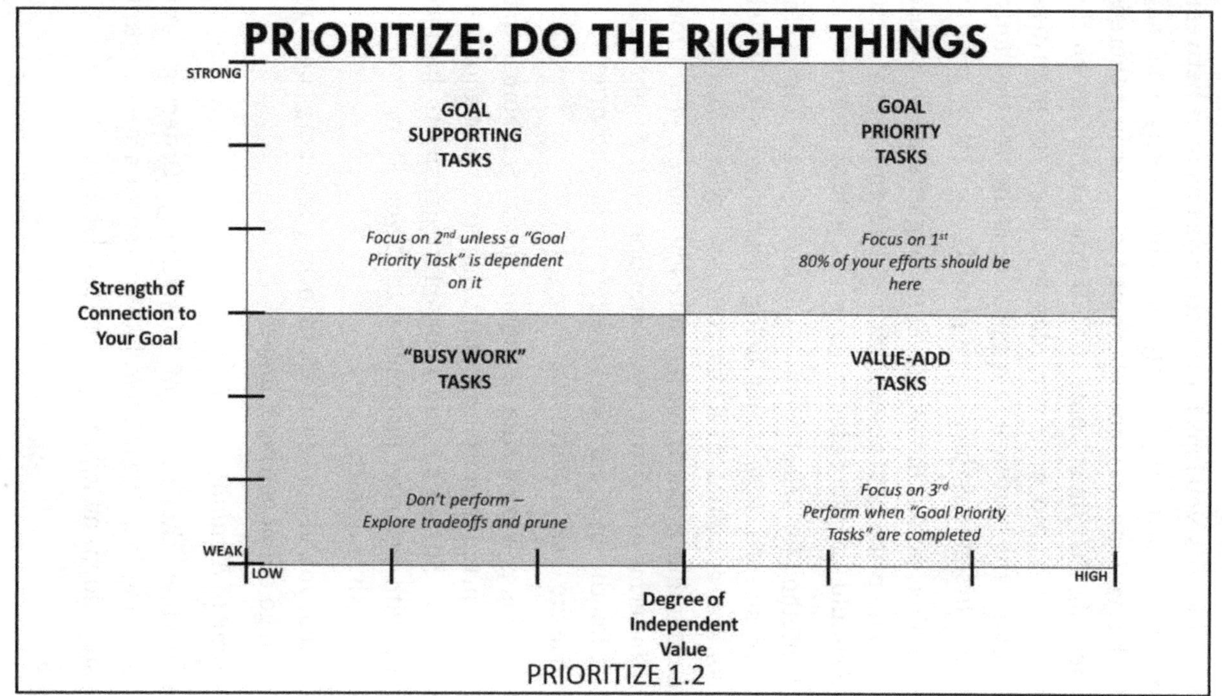

PRIORITIZE 1.2

In other words, you look for the strongest balance between *order* and *priority*. If you only focus on priority, you may find that you cannot complete some tasks, because there is something that must come first. If you only focus on the what must come first, you may lose sight of priorities. Therefore, the best task to begin with is the one that must be done first and is the highest priority.

Remember, action builds power through iteration, so use order and priority to guide which activity to start with, but you should still worry more about just getting started.

This method for selecting the right task to start with is not a hard science. It is about being intentional with which tasks and activities to focus your energy on. The act of ordering and prioritizing has already moved you a long way in terms of focusing your attention on the right tasks. Look for the best balance between order and priority to choose the task to start with.

While this is a good rule of thumb, please remember that getting started is more important than worrying about the right task. So, if you find yourself struggling to balance order with priority, just pick a task you know you can accomplish and start.

Now that you've chosen a task to focus your energy on, how do you go about getting it done?

It's time to *Escalate*.

To review the steps of Unpacking, Ordering, and Prioritizing, visit the full Escalate course for access to step-by-step videos at kylebrost.com/escalate.

Why it works:

a. *Refer to Chapter 7: Be Undaunted from the Start. Prioritizing keeps your attention focused on the small and simple actions that will produce results. Whenever stalled, you can use priority to determine the next practical action.*

b. *Refer to Chapter 14: Keep Your Purpose Front and Center. It's easy to lose sight of your goal through all of the activities required to get there. Prioritizing connects each of your tasks to your larger goal and purpose. Rather than seeing those tasks as individual elements, you see them as part of your purpose, and this is energizing.*

c. *Refer to Chapter 13: Pare Down Your Decisions. Similar to ordering, prioritizing pares down your decisions. Rather than choosing between hundreds of tasks, your choices are narrowed down to a select few, this paring down of decisions makes it easier to direct attention toward the right ones.*

d. *Refer to Chapter 10: Stop Habits From Killing Your Goals. Prioritizing your activities forces you to acknowledge where your habits are preventing you from doing the right actions. As you explore your own habits and compare them to your priorities, you'll see where there are gaps and new habits need to be developed.*

STEP #2: ESCALATE

With your foundation set through unpacking, ordering, and prioritizing you are now ready to leverage the first tool to get unstuck. You are ready to *Escalate*.

THE RULES:

1) **YOU WANT ESCALATE AN ACTIVITY EVERY TIME IT FAILS**
2) **EVERY ESCALATION MUST BE PAID FOR**
3) **YOU CAN ONLY ESCALATE A MAXIMUM OF 3 TIMES**

As you select tasks to perform, you need to decide how you will accomplish them. This may seem obvious, and you're thinking, "I just do it, right?" If it were that simple, you wouldn't be stuck, and you wouldn't need my help.

Don't get me wrong, if you're driven and can take action right away, then stop reading and do it. However, you may look at the activities that need to be done and feel your heart start to race as anxiety, worry, frustration, or any number of emotions flood. You're not excited about the activity you must do, or, even worse, you flat out dread it!

Not to worry, learning to *Escalate* will keep you moving, even when you dread activities. I recommend the seven methods below to accomplish any given task. They progress from the simplest to the most complex.

This list is not comprehensive, the *ActionHacks* contains a more comprehensive list of methods. However, experience with my clients has shown that the seven methods listed below are all one really needs.

Remember, one component of developing desire is to recognize there is method for achieving your goal. These methods when applied correctly will do just that.

LIST OF ESCALATIONS (METHODS)

Escalation 1: The 5-Minute Approach. Use this *escalation* for the most basic of tasks. Look for a task that will take less than five minutes to complete and then complete that task. This is easy to start with because you know going in that you will not be spending more than five minutes on it.

Escalation 2: The 10-Minute Approach. Use this *escalation* for tasks that you do not want to do or are procrastinating on. Commit to 10 minutes of working on the task, when the 10 minutes are up, give yourself permission to stop. You will be surprised how much progress you can make just 10 minutes at a time. As long as you hold yourself accountable to this rule on a regular basis, you will continue to make progress.

Escalation 3: The Power Session. Use this *escalation* when the 5-Minute and 10-Minute *escalations* are either unsuccessful or not a choice. Power sessions are specific blocks of time set apart to work intensely on completing a task. They can range from 1-4 hour blocks of time and require creating the right environment to stay focused.

Escalation 4: Accountability & Rewards. Use this *escalation* when you have not carried out prior Escalations as you said you would. It involves creating accountability and rewarding yourself when you do make progress, no matter how small the achievement. Start by holding yourself accountable and rewarding whether or not you DO *escalations* 1-3, whether or not those *escalations* achieve your desired results. This is key because the only thing you can control is your effort, not the results.

Escalation 5: Collaboration. When Escalations 1-3 either will not or have not worked, then you need to find someone to collaborate with. There are several reasons you may need to *escalate* a task to collaboration. The first is when Escalations 1-3 have not got you to your goal, and you therefore need someone to hold you accountable.

This form of collaboration involves finding someone who will hold you responsible for completing a task and allowing them to do so. Second is when you don't have the skill or capability to accomplish a job but need to participate or learn it. In this case, you should find someone who has the willingness and expertise to collaborate with you. Most often in power session format, you would invite them to work with you for a specific block (or blocks) of time to accomplish a task. Collaborations work well for clearly defined tasks that need either accountability or an additional level of expertise and capability that you do not possess.

Escalation 6: Outsource. There are three primary reasons to outsource, the first being that you have repeatedly failed to complete the task on your own. The second is that you need it done quickly. And finally, someone else can do it better, more efficiently, and for less money than you can yourself.

Escalation 7: Partnership. A partnership is a formal ongoing or long-term agreement where both parties agree to perform a specific set of responsibilities. The distinction between Collaboration and Partnership is the formality and duration.

Where collaboration has either failed or is not a good fit, you should consider escalating the activity to partnership. The distinction between collaboration and partnership is the nature of the task.

For tasks that are short-term and finite, collaboration is most suitable. For tasks that are long-term, ongoing, or indefinite, partnership is often the better choice. You should never form a partnership for a one-off, temporary, or very minor task. Partnerships should be reserved for extremely high priority tasks that will need to be repeated many times in the future.

For a printable copy of the escalations, visit kylebrost.com/escalate

As you consider the options for completing any given task, you will see that they advance from the simplest to the most complex. When you are dreading an activity, start with the simplest and DO NOT underestimate the power of small and simple things to bring about massive accomplishment!

To *Escalate* is simple. But before you *Escalate,* you must start. Select the activity you will accomplish and the timeframe you will complete it in. Next, determine a budget for that activity, this is an actual dollar amount you believe the activity is worth.

You should also assign a total budget for the goal. After that, begin with one of the first three methods on the list and use it to complete the task.

If your chosen method works, meaning you do it and complete the task within your timeframe, you don't need to *Escalate.* Move on to the next task based on *order* and *priority.*

Some methods will fail, and when they do, you want to *Escalate.* If you don't carry out the activity, that is a failure and reason to *Escalate.* Likewise, if you start the task but do not complete it within your timeframe that is another reason to *Escalate.*

Anytime a method fails, you *Escalate* to the next most powerful method for completing the task. You do not get to retry *Escalations*; if you do that, you will remain stuck.

Let's say Alexander's task was to draft an email message to individuals who have found an apparel manufacturer before, and he chose the *power session* approach to start. He blocks out two hours on his calendar to draft the messages. When the allotted time comes around, he meanders down to his office, looks around at the mess, then sits down on the couch.

He thinks, "Well, I have two hours to do this, it'll probably only take 30 minutes. I should probably watch some videos on the funniest emails before I start." Soon, he's in a YouTube spiral watching intense nature scenes mixed with laughing babies. And before he knows it, his time is up. That was a failure! (And yes, this has happened!)

Remember, the first rule of *Escalation* states that whenever a selected method fails to complete the task or make sufficient progress on it, you want to *Escalate* to the next level... every time. There is no, "I'll try it again at this same level," you either make enough progress, or you don't. If you don't, then you *Escalate*, no excuses!

Since Alexander's *power session* didn't work, he now *escalates* to the next method, which is *Escalation 4: Accountability & Rewards.* This escalation says that you need some level of accountability or reward to encourage completion of the task. Here is the catch though, escalating does not come for free.

The purpose of escalating your efforts is to ensure you don't repeat the same actions hoping for different results. In this way, you solidify your commitment to achievement and build persistence.

When you let yourself fruitlessly repeat efforts that haven't worked, you will end up in a downward spiral resulting in being stuck. However, when you escalate your commitment to achieve your goal grows and your ability to persist becomes habit.

Why it works:

a. *Refer to Chapter 3: Take Action Today to Ensure Action Tomorrow. If what you try doesn't work, you only have two options, give up or try something different. Action is all you have, so keep using what you have by continuing to take action. Escalation ensures that you continue to leverage your most valuable resource, action.*

b. *Refer to Chapter 4: Don't Look for a Map, Build Your Own Along the Way. It's difficult to predict how the journey to your goal will go. By escalating, you ensure that you build the map along the way. It's okay if your first attempt isn't the right one, you escalate and build a new waypoint on your map to goal achievement*

c. *Refer to Chapter 11: Create Goal-oriented Action Chains. Many people's default action chain when an effort fails, is to pause and even stop. By escalating you build a new default action chain. Instead of pausing or stopping, you escalate. This not only prevents you from getting stuck, but it also accelerates your achievement and builds lifelong momentum.*

As mentioned though, escalating isn't free. Whenever a method is ineffective, you must pay for it.

This is the second rule of escalation; whenever you *escalate* from one method to another, you must pay for it. You pay for escalation either with money, with your time/effort, or with service. Therefore, you set a budget up front to pay for these escalations (and to reward yourself when you successfully complete a task).

This commitment involves putting money aside based on your assessed value of that activity. You should perform some research to find out what it would cost to have someone else perform the task.

In Alexander's example, the budget he set for the activity was $45 because a quick internet search revealed several providers who could complete it for that amount. However, because he failed to complete the task, he pays $15 of that money to *escalate* the activity.

The reason it costs $15 to escalate this activity is that the total budget for it is $45. Assuming a worst-case scenario of having to *escalate* three times, you divide the total budget by three. So, $45 divided by three potential escalations is $15. This way, you still have money in your budget if you must *escalate* two more times.

Whenever you pay for an escalation, the money comes out of the total budget for the goal. Alexander's total budget for launching his apparel company was $5,000, but that is now reduced to a total of $5,985 because of the $15 paid for escalating.

The money paid for escalations is literally set aside. You place it in an envelope, transfer it to a separate account, or even give it to another person to hold onto.

Paying for escalations is a mechanism of accountability. By recognizing that missed action doesn't come free, it is a poignant reminder to take the small and simple steps necessary to make progress. When you pay for escalations, you accept accountability and build greater persistence in carrying out future escalations.

It's important to note that paying for escalations is not about punishment! It is not punishment to ensure you make progress on your goals. Payment is not about punishing yourself for failure, it's about inspiring yourself to take more action in creative ways.

This is about your accountability to progress and to who you are becoming. Paying for escalations also elicits your creativity.

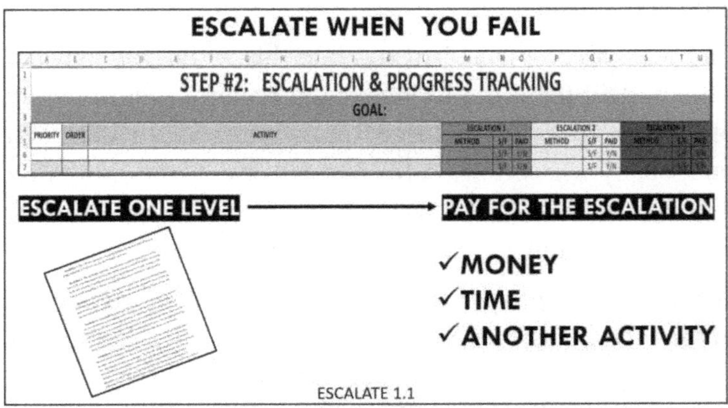

ESCALATE 1.1

If you do not have a budget or you have exceeded the budget, you need to pay for every escalation in an alternative way. If you don't have the money to pay for it, you need to give time, effort, or service.

I usually hear something like this at this point, "How does paying for escalation with effort actually work?"

The answer is simple; you choose an unrelated task that you know you will complete because there is no barrier to you doing it. This is usually something you're good at and don't mind doing (or maybe even enjoy doing), and you trade that effort for either money (i.e., you get paid for it) or you can ask someone to trade that activity for one you need to get done but haven't carried out yourself.

Maybe you've been trying to proofread a lengthy document but need to *escalate* it. Offer to do a service for friends or family members in exchange for their help. You could try offering something to your social network and see who is interested in swapping their skills in a mutually beneficial way.

Or you could check out the website www.simbi.com, which matches people who want to swap their services. Last, you can trade time from somewhere else to do this, for example, you may decide to wake up 30 minutes earlier to complete an unrelated task as a payment of accountability.

The purpose of paying for escalations is not just a practical one. In terms of ensuring there are resources enough to complete it, it is also one of discipline. When you allow yourself to fail repeatedly without any accountability, it becomes easier and easier to get stuck.

Just because you may not have a budget to pay for escalations, don't let it slide, find a way to pay for your escalations to ensure progress.

THE POWER OF SERVICE

The effects of service cannot be emphasized enough. It's no secret that giving, serving, and volunteering all make you happier. However, as humans, we tend to devalue what that means.

Research shows that weekly service produces an increase in happiness comparable to an income increase of $50,000-$70,000![25]

Not only does service make you happier, but as a result, you have higher levels of purpose and self-confidence and lower levels of anxiety. These factors are crucial to getting started, maintaining momentum, and combating negativity and stress.

Even more, depending on the service, you can stay physically active and build beneficial social connections. While not directly associated with momentum, these elements have serious benefits to your overall health. And you never know who you'll meet! Maybe a great accountability partner or collaborator.

There are many ways to serve. I have an employee that finds an hour trip to the local animal shelter can reinvigorate an otherwise unproductive day. You might find that you love reading to kids or helping someone learn English.

If you don't have the schedule for a fixed program, try something flexible or perform simple acts of kindness like picking up garbage or writing an encouraging note to someone.

An off-the-cuff approach can be just as worthwhile, but you should also set aside time for it. If you don't schedule time for it, it will fall by the wayside and you will miss out on the benefits.

Whatever it is, make sure that it is something that you can commit to and that carries meaning for you.

This is the hidden power in paying for escalations, creativity. Paying for your escalation enlists your creative energy. And, yes! You are creative!

Studies have shown that when your options are narrowed, your creativity actually increases. When options are unlimited, you're not forced to consider resources and possibilities from multiple perspectives. However, when options and resources are limited, it forces you to consider new and innovative ways to accomplish tasks.

Paying for escalations recruits the creative power that is within you.

Consider Kimberly Causey, who didn't have the resources to get her book idea, a furnishings buying guide, printed. Rather than give up and get stuck, she recruited her creativity. She used her limited resources, paying $200 to have book covers professionally printed. She then printed the book's pages one at a time on her home printer, folded and scored the covers, and used a hot glue gun and butter knife to glue the books together.

Kimberly eventually turned her creatively printed furniture buying guide into the go-to resource for interior decorators.

Or take Todd Staples who had stalled with his business Stealth Auto. Feeling like he had no money or resources to progress, he volunteered to be on the show *Fear Factor*. He appeared three times and won $50,000. Getting the worst of it, he had to eat something nasty all three times, including pizza with bile based sauce.

Todd used these uniquely obtained funds to get his business unstuck, becoming a thriving venture.

When you pay for your escalations, you will unleash your creativity, finding better solutions to your challenges and getting yourself unstuck in surprising ways.

When you pay for escalations, you encourage the completion of future tasks and begin to build momentum, no matter how you pay for it.

Why it works:

a. *Refer to Chapter 12: Make it Easy to Do. Along your journey toward goal achievement, you will inevitably try something that doesn't work. When this happens, recovery can be difficult. However, by paying for it initially, you make recovering and moving forward easier to do in the future. Rather than scrapping for resources, you will already have them in place or you will have identified potential ways to get them.*

b. *Refer to Chapter 3: Take Action Today to Ensure You Act Tomorrow. When your effort fails to produce results, it can feel like a shot to the gut (and your pride). By immediately paying for it though, you have taken action. Even if that action appears to be unrelated to your goal, action perpetuates action, and paying enlists this force.*

The third rule is that you can only *escalate* a maximum of three times. What happens when you've used three escalations, and the task still isn't completed? You move directly to *Escalation #6: Outsource.*

If you have followed the rules, you will have money set aside for outsourcing. This is why you pay each time you escalate, to ensure that there are enough resources to keep you moving forward.

There are innumerable options for outsourcing work, and it doesn't matter what the activity is, you can find someone to support you. Whether you are working on a personal goal, a professional one, or an organizational one, there is no excuse for not being able to outsource.

From folding laundry to drafting business models, hanging pictures to business valuations, someone is ready and qualified to do it. And more than likely for much less than you might expect.

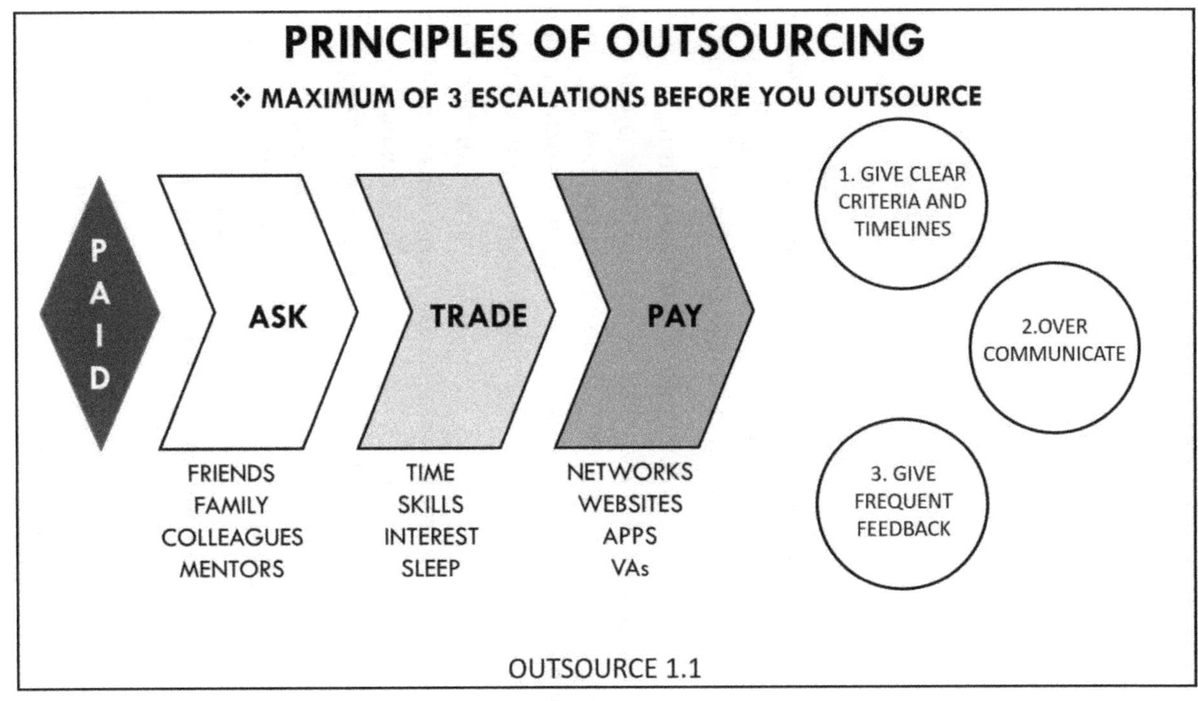

OUTSOURCE 1.1

A list of ways to outsource work

- Ask friends, family, or coworkers
- Ask your social networks
- Ask for referrals from friends, family, coworkers, and social networks

Use a website, such as:

www.freeeup.com

www.fiverr.com

www.fancyhands.com

www.upwork.com

www.99designs.com

www.freelancer.com

www.toptal.com

www.peopleperhour.com

www.guru.com

Use an App or Service:

www.taskrabbit.com

www.takl.com

www.handy.com

www.thumbtack.com

Work with a Virtual Assistant or VA Organization:

www.wow24-7.io

www.mytasker.com

www.intelligentoffice.com

www.vatalks.com

www.worldwide101.com

www.noondalton.com

www.avirtual.co.uk

www.virtualassistusa.com

www.magellan-solutions.com

www.taskvirtual.com

There are many reasons the process of *Escalate* is effective. First, by escalating things to outsource after only three attempts, you are guaranteed to keep making efficient progress on your goal. When you don't escalate to outsource, you may spend weeks, months, or even years stalled by that one activity. When all you needed was it done so you could focus on other tasks.

It is misleading to think that you must personally complete every task en route to achieving a goal. No matter the target, you will require the support and assistance of others.

It does not diminish the accomplishment of a goal when you get the support of others. Even if that support comes in the form of outsourcing. Would you rather remain stuck, but be able to say you got stuck all by yourself? Or accomplish your goal and share how you found support to accomplish it?

Second, if you attempt one or two *escalations* and complete the task, you now have money set aside for a reward or other budgeted items. Remember, rewards are effective at shaping future behavior. By using the time/effort budgeting technique, you either assure yourself that you have money to outsource or you provide yourself with a nice reward when tasks are completed.

Last, when you chose to pay for outsourcing through effort, you continue to develop the willpower to take action and build momentum. If you were able to *escalate* any task to outsource without consequence, you wouldn't develop the ability to get unstuck and take action. Whereas, if every time you *Escalate* an activity, you must pay for it, and sometimes with added effort or resourcefulness, you are still getting yourself into motion.

Do you recall the message from earlier chapters? Getting yourself into motion is vital, you can point yourself in the right direction later. So, even if the effort you use to pay for escalations isn't related to your goal, you still got yourself into motion and took action to move closer to that goal. The more you do this, the more natural taking action will become.

Holding yourself accountable is a great life skill you can apply to any aspect of life. Take my colleague who followed the *Escalate* process to lose weight. When she failed in the 10-minute method, she escalated to accountability and rewards and later to collaboration.

Each time she escalated her activity, she committed to cleaning a friend's house and folding her laundry in return for a $25 payment. After three escalations, she reached outsourcing. By cleaning her friend's house and doing her laundry after each escalation, she had earned $75 and set it aside as payment. Her $75 was enough money to hire a personal trainer for five sessions. And those five sessions got her moving towards her goal.

How you crunch the numbers or define the effort is up to you, but you want to pay for *escalations*. When paying for them out of a budget, there are implications for how much money will be available for other activities. While paying for them with effort requires taking additional action.

The main point is to get yourself into action. By needing to pay with money or effort for *escalations*, you ensure progress is made toward your goal. It gets you into motion, even if the direction isn't pointed toward your goal.

Once you're in motion, you'll find it's easier to redirect your actions toward the goal you outlined. The combination of outsourcing when necessary, and paying for it along the way, is powerful. It ensures both progress and increased future ability to take action.

There is criticism that relying on outsourcing won't improve your ability to take action. This is true if all you ever do is outsource. Doing so means you don't build the capability to take action. However, experience shows that most activities do not get outsourced.

Typically, two *escalations* will produce results, and therefore will not reach the point of outsourcing. While you may rely on outsourcing at the start of your project when you feel stuck or without momentum, it's likely that you will depend on it less as your project continues.

As you are spurred into action, your desire and willpower will increase, and you will rely less on outsourcing. Second, you will get better at recognizing what is best to outsource. This will improve your results.

Another common objection to outsourcing is that it is somehow evidence of failure. This couldn't be further from the truth; it is evidence of a commitment to your goals. Would you rather outsource and accomplish your goal or fail at your goal because you were too proud to ask for support?

The irony for many of my clients who raise this objection is that they raise it while I'm with them in the room. This objection quickly dissolves when I politely point out I'm a consultant who they have essentially *outsourced* to! If you want to accomplish your goal, don't let the pride of doing it alone stop you.

If you are still concerned that you are relying on outsourcing too much, it helps to remember the Pareto Principle, which states that 80% of your results will come from 20% of your efforts. In achieving any goal, a select few actions truly impact the achievement of your goal.

If your attention is focused on the value-producing 20% of effort that leads to 80% of your goal, then how the rest gets done isn't critical. Remember, the other 80% of effort will only produce an additional 20% of value. If you've unpacked, ordered, and prioritized effectively, you'll be able to identify the 20% that will produce 80% of the results.

Even when things are outsourced, you build momentum. Outsourcing serves as a mechanism to get things done. It also encourages you to put your money (or your effort) where your mouth is and frees up your attention to focus on activities that you can complete independently.

There is something incredibly powerful about seeing action in any form (even outsourcing) move you toward a goal. This clear progress inspires more action.

One source for outsourcing has recognized this, and after each purchase, they email their receipts with the clever subject line: "Here's your receipt of doing."

For a full list of outsourcing tools including The Effective Outsourcing Checklist, access the *Escalate* Course online at kylebrost.com/escalate

Why it works:

a. *Refer to Chapter 9: Don't Dare to Start Over. The number one consideration to outsourcing is that it prevents you from starting over, it guarantees progress. Don't get stuck because you're unwilling to move forward a different way, Don't Dare to Start Over, outsource.*

b. *Refer to Chapter 5: Leverage Your Most Powerful Tool, Progress. When you outsource you ensure progress and that progress is exciting. By seeing progress toward your goal, even via outsourcing, you will be energized to keep pushing forward.*

c. *Refer to Chapter 6: Strive For Potential, Not Validation. The reason many people resist outsourcing is because they are seeking validation. They perceive outsourcing as a statement about their potential (i.e., If I have to outsource, I'm a failure). By outsourcing, you not only place achievement of your goal as the top priority, but you also acknowledge that you don't need validation, you need potential. Outsourcing is simply evidence that you have greater potential to reach.*

STEP #3: PRUNING

One of the most effective ways of directing your energy, money, and time toward your goals, is to say "no". Pruning is the process by which you consciously choose what you won't do.

THE RULES:

- YOUR GOAL REMAINS INTACT, WHILE YOUR APPROACH IS FLEXIBLE

The final step you need is *pruning*. When you started this process, you captured a lot of tasks that needed to be carried out. However, not all of those activities must be done. They may be reasonable but not required.

The first round of defense against these unnecessary tasks is to order and prioritize. However, there are times when unnecessary activities still make it through and slow your progress. Pruning is the second layer of defense against these progress-destroying activities.

Sometimes you become stuck because you are too focused on a task that does not need to be done. You feel guilty for not doing it but can't seem to complete it. This reinforcing spiral of guilt and not getting it done can lead you to give up a goal altogether.

If you have tried your hardest to unpack, order, prioritize, and *Escalate*, but to no avail, it is time to prune. Or, if you feel like there are too many things to do, it is time to prune.

Pruning involves changing tasks to work on other activities and then testing the impact. Many times, you will find that the problematic activity doesn't need to be done. When you cannot make progress on an activity, prune it and try moving forward.

Pruning is also a powerful tool to combat perfectionism. If you suffer from paralysis by analysis, you can overcome this sense of perfection by pruning. Move forward and see if it is as big a deal as your inner doubt tells you.

Many times, you'll discover that it wasn't a big deal at all.

You have limited resources, whether physical, emotional, or intellectual. The better you get at directing those resources toward your goals, the better you'll be at achieving them. Pruning is about saying "no" to those things that stand in the way of your goals, no matter how innocent they may seem.

One individual I worked with had stalled on producing an educational video because he couldn't get himself to script it out. He believed that scripting the video was crucial. However, when I encouraged him to prune this activity and just shoot the video, the end result was a more natural and powerful video than what he would have scripted.

While scripting the video was a reasonable task, it was unnecessary and getting him stuck. Pruning this task got him unstuck and moving toward his goal.

If it is indeed a necessary activity, you can bring it back later. If it's not needed, you'll be able to make progress by moving past it. The only time I would deter you from pruning is if cutting an activity would dramatically impact your goal. In that case, you need to persevere.

A notable example of this involves the tasks identified earlier for Alexander's apparel business. Two tasks identified were research payment processing and select a payment processor. What would be the impact if he skipped researching payment processing and moved directly to selecting a payment processor?

While researching payment processing may have made it onto the list of tasks, if he had become stalled at this spot, he could have disregarded researching payment processing and moved directly to selecting a payment processor. He would likely find that this task is not as critical as assumed.

There are certainly tradeoffs to pruning some tasks, but which is the greater tradeoff? Potentially higher vendor rates or getting stuck and not having any revenue to worry about vendor rates?

Once again, it is worth considering the Pareto Principle as you decide which activities to prune. It's a great mental exercise to ask which tasks are part of the 20% that produce 80% of the value, and which fall into the 80% that generate just 20% of the progress you need.

Pruning is a useful way to weed out the unnecessary activities for the sake of progress. Often, you'll be surprised at how few activities are required to accomplish a goal.

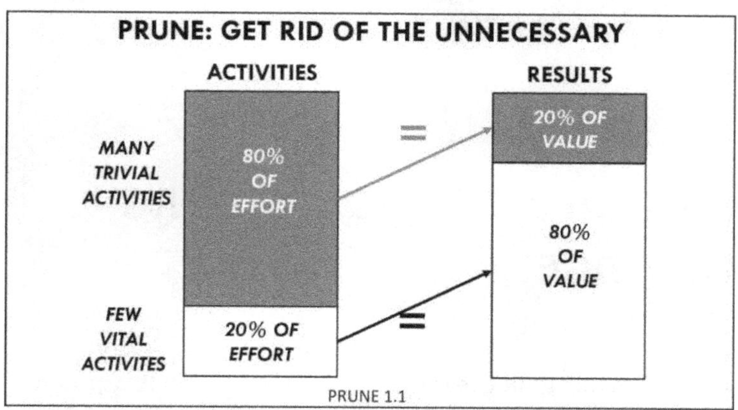

PRUNE 1.1

Why it works:

a. *Refer to Chapter 13: Pare Down Your Decisions. Through pruning, you literally pare down your decisions. You remove decisions that fall into the 80% of effort that only produces 20% of your results. The pruning process gives you structure and guidance on how to do it effectively.*

b. *Refer to Chapter 4: Don't Look for a Map, Build Your Own Along the Way. When building a map, you need to identify what needs to be on the map, as well as what does not need to be on the map. Pruning gives clarity to your course by removing the unnecessary waypoints.*

SECTION 3: PUT ESCALATE INTO PRACTICE

Whether your goal is to start a business, lose a few pounds, or become one of the top McDonald's franchises in the country, the *Escalate* process with its principles of action is sure to get you there.

The complete process of *Escalate* works because it offers options for how you get work done, starting with even the smallest and simplest things like The 5-Minute Approach. In turn, it ensures you continue moving forward, even when you can't seem to get yourself out of a rut.

It naturally overcomes the classic definition of insanity, which is to repeat the same actions over and over, expecting different results. The moment an effort does not work, you *Escalate*.

Think big, take action, and when in doubt, summon your inner Cordia Harrington. Small steps really do accomplish great things.

THE SIX CORE PRINCIPLES OF ESCALATE

1. **Unpack your big goal into smaller more manageable tasks before you start**
2. **Determine the order that those tasks should be completed**
3. **Identify the highest priority tasks**
4. **Escalate your efforts by choosing more powerful ways of getting things done when an approach has not worked**
5. **Pay for your escalations intentionally and willingly**
6. **Outsource when you get stuck**
7. **Consciously choose what you will NOT do by pruning unnecessary activities**
8. **Repeat steps 1-6 until you achieve your goal then start on a new one!**

Watch a Q&A video defining and clarifying each step of the escalate process in the full Escalate Course at kylebrost.com/escalate

BONUS: 23 Action Hacks Proven to Beat Procrastination

Download the ActionHacks at kylebrost.com/escalate

Can't wait to take Action? This section reviews everything we have covered in the book: lessons learned from Cordia Harrington, the Action + Desire = Progress equation, how action perpetuates action, progress is power, extraordinary is a behavior not a result, failure is evidence of greater potential, as well as the Escalation process. These additional and useful hacks help you plan and execute your goals and make day-to-day progress.

#1: CHANGE YOUR THINKING

The first way to get yourself to take action is ultra simple and incredibly intuitive, it is to change your thinking. Stop thinking about how hard or undesirable the activity is. Stop telling yourself that you need motivation. Repeat in your mind or out loud, "Do it. Do it now. Do it! Do it!" Remind yourself that Action + Desire = Progress and the fact that you are even debating whether to do the activity or not is evidence that you have the desire, you just need the action.

Remind yourself that even a small, simple action toward your goal is a massive success.

#2: VISUALIZATION

Every successful goal starts with a vision of what success looks like. Allow yourself to visualize that goal, imagine what it will be like to accomplish it, the feelings you will have and the power of that moment. Then, imagine completing the task at hand: visualize what it will feel like to complete that task, reflect on what it will mean to see progress. Use visualization as a stepping stone to action.

#3: SELF-AFFIRMATIONS

Self-affirmations are different than traditional affirmations, which ask you to state things you desire to be. Instead of focusing on things you desire to be, self-affirmations encourage you to think about things you value. So, rather than looking in the mirror and telling yourself, "I'm amazing, I can do this!" you say out loud or in your head things related to true values of yours such as, "I value results" or "I value accomplishment." The key to using self-affirmations as an ActionHack is to identify authentic values that encourage the completion of tasks. For example, one person may use the self-affirmation of "I value results" because it is authentic to them. While another person may use the self-affirmation of "I value accomplishing difficult things." Choose a value that is genuine and authentic and that encourages the completion of tasks and repeat that affirmation to yourself.

#4: WRITE IT DOWN

Research has shown repeatedly that writing things down, especially longhand with a pen and paper, increases your commitment to the idea and to taking action. Find a pen and paper and write down your commitment to completing the task at hand. Then, review and reflect on this commitment until you complete the task. It will be incredibly difficult to review and reflect on this commitment repeatedly without making progress on the task. Besides, the simple act of writing it down solidifies your commitment to it.

#5: THE FIRST THING

Do something meaningful first thing in the morning. How often do you start your day with social media or email and before you know it, you're lost in low-value tasks? How you start your day can set the direction for the remainder of it. So, choose one meaningful activity that will take 10-15 minutes to complete, and start your day with that. Beginning with control and focus will set you up for success.

#6: THE ONE THING

Identify the one thing that you MUST do today and don't end your day until you've done it. Doing this one thing will ensure that no matter what else happens during the day, you will have completed your most important task. Forcing yourself to narrow it down to one thing ensures that you prioritize. You can't do everything, so you have to prioritize what is most important.

#7: THEME YOUR DAYS

When you have similar sets of activities that need to be performed through the week or month, it can be useful to theme your days. This involves focusing on a specific "theme" or group of activities on specific days. For example, you may theme Mondays as "Preparation" days, meaning that on Monday you focus your attention on getting everything ready and organized for the rest of the week. Then, you might theme Tuesdays as "Outreach," so on Tuesdays, you would focus your attention on emailing and calling targets and associates. You choose the themes, but by focusing on a specific theme, you can better align your work within any given day, which will encourage focus.

#8: UNPACK IT

Take the big goal that you have in mind and unpack it into small, manageable tasks. Focus your attention on completing those tasks. It's easier to focus attention on small, doable tasks than something large that feels overwhelming.

#9: 2-MINUTE RULE

Do any significant activity that will take less than two minutes immediately. Don't wait, don't hesitate, do it now. If it will take less than two minutes to accomplish and you don't get it done, you might ask yourself if it needs to be done.

#10: 5-MINUTE RULE

Consider your goal and then identify a specific task that can be accomplished in five minutes. Set the timer and complete that one small task.

#11: 10-MINUTE RULE

For an activity that you need to do, but don't want to do, set a timer for 10 minutes and work on it until the timer goes off. When the timer goes off, give yourself permission to be done. Working on the task in 10-minute increments. Often, you'll find that a few minutes into the task, you no longer have the desire to stop because getting started is the hardest part. Feel free to continue to work on it in 10-minute increments until it is completed. This is especially useful for tasks that leave you prone to procrastination.

#12: MAKE IT EASY

Make the tasks that you want to get done, easy to do. We are good at creating barriers to things we want to avoid, like removing all the junk food from the house when we're on a diet. But we rarely spend as much time making the things we want to do, easy to do. Ask yourself, what can I do to make this activity easier? Can you lay out all of the materials beforehand? Can you reserve the right space?

#13: MEASURE PROGRESS

If you want to sustain action, you need to see your progress. Make a checklist of simple actions you'll take today, those things you'll do that lead you toward your goals. As you do each one, cross it off the list. This will help you see and acknowledge that you are in fact making progress. Each time you check something off the list, you will gain a sense of satisfaction and feel compelled to check another task off the list. You can also leave completed items on your desk until later so that you can see the progress you're making.

#14: GET CREATIVE

Sometimes it's not taking action that presents the problem; it's some small component of an activity. When this happens, choose an activity that may not seem directly related, but which has the potential to contribute. Need to do some research, but hate researching? Try watching a movie that loosely relates to the topic and document ideas while you do. Need to design a template for a project? Buy a puzzle of architecture and document ideas while you complete it. Once you get into motion, you often discover that it doesn't matter what direction you were headed in when you started, you can now steer yourself in the right direction.

#15: POWER SESSION

Don't make a project out of something that doesn't need to be a project. Don't form a committee or launch an initiative for things that with concerted action could be solved in one sitting. Instead of planning out steps, set aside a specific block of time, typically between 2-6 hours to power through it. Focus that time exclusively on completing that task and nothing else—and I mean nothing else. Need to redesign your website? Try a Power Session. Need a new process for client engagement? Try a Power Session. You'll be amazed at how much progress you make and how quickly Power Sessions replace projects as the norm, rather than the exception.

#16: REWARD YOURSELF

Rewards are more effective than punishment. So, before you jump to punishing yourself for not following through on commitments, try rewarding yourself for your successes. Always wanted to try that sushi bar down the road, get the royal treatment at the spa, or catch a game from behind home plate? Set some success criteria and reward yourself when you've followed through. The great thing about rewards is that they don't even have to be big to be effective, even small rewards like an extended lunch break or a printed certificate can be powerful.

#17: CREATE ACCOUNTABILITY

Make yourself accountable by sharing your goals and commitments with others. When you make commitments publicly and write them down, you become more responsible to them. Sometimes, merely sharing them with others will be enough. Other times, you will need to give someone else permission to hold you accountable. This requires allowing them to call you out on missed commitments. To assist with this, you may give them some power, like your Netflix or social media password which they can change when you don't follow through on commitments. You can also give this person permission to reward you.

A SIDE NOTE: One creative way to enlist accountability is to make a bet. Choose a buddy and tell them the activity you will complete and the timeline. Commit to doing something for them if you do not complete it within that timeline. A few examples include buying them breakfast or lunch, taking them to a movie, or even giving them $10.

#18: COLLABORATE

You don't have to go it alone. Sometimes the only thing you need to move forward is the support and expertise of another person. If an activity feels just outside of your comfort zone or expertise, consider collaborating with another person. Collaboration builds on accountability by creating a natural form of responsibility. Additionally, it gives you access to information and resources that you wouldn't have going it alone. The biggest barrier to collaboration is often pride, but would you rather have your pride or your progress?

#19: OUTSOURCE

You should consider outsourcing activities for a variety of reasons. If an activity is outside your skill or knowledge, could be performed much more efficiently and effectively by another person, or is just not happening on your watch, bring in reinforcements! There's no shame in outsourcing your work for the sake of progress, especially with access to a global workforce through technology. You may be surprised to learn how many activities can be outsourced; there's virtually no limit.

Outsourcing to Technology: Not all outsourcing must go to a person. The world is filled with technologies that can serve critical functions for you. It is wise to explore what technologies you can outsource to, in addition to people.

#20: PARTNER UP

When you repeatedly find yourself relying on Collaboration and Outsourcing to get similar items completed, it may be time to consider a more formal and structured Partnership. The advantages to Partnering Up are that you can brainstorm, learn from each other, set contractual expectations, negotiate special rates, and grow together.

#21: BUILD UP CAPABILITY

As you work through all available options for getting things done and sustaining momentum, you should be asking, "How am I building capability?" To build capability is to personally (or organizationally) develop the skill and expertise to accomplish the task as well as anyone. This is not as critical for one-off and ad hoc activities, but for those activities that are strategic to you and your business, you should be building Capability while you rely on other methods in the interim. The long-term solution for any vital activity is to be competent at executing it.

BONUS: AUDIT YOUR TIME

Tracking how you spend your time can be phenomenally eye-opening, but few people do it. If you're stuck, one of the most useful things you can do is to perform a time audit. Track your time for 3-7 days, taking notes about what you did and how you feel about the time spent. After you have completed the tracking, review it. This will make your successes and your struggles visible. It will also help you identify patterns, bottlenecks, and tendencies you will want to either encourage or discourage.

BONUS: TAKE A PROCRASTINATION FAST

A procrastination fast is a simple and powerful way to discover how good it feels to take action. Fasting is a willing abstinence or reduction of some item, typically food.

However, in a procrastination fast, you are abstaining (going without) from procrastination. It's easier than you might think. For 30 days, you wake up and write down one thing you've been procrastinating. Then, you do that one thing. These can be simple things, like writing a letter to a loved one, canceling that old subscription you never use, etc. Simply choose one thing each day that you've been putting off and get it done. Do this for 30 days and you'll find your ability to get unstuck and build momentum has grown dramatically.

HELP OTHERS ESCALATE

Escalate is a simple yet powerful process for getting you unstuck and building lifelong momentum. However, it's not something to do alone. While the process focuses on your own actions and progress, it is at the same time dependent on your ability to collaborate and partner with others.

There is no outsourcing, accountability, collaboration, or partnership without the support of others. As you begin your own journey to *Escalate*, help others do the same.

First, share the principles of action and escalation with them. When you see them stalled and backing away from a goal, encourage them to rapidly increase their efforts in intensity and magnitude. Offer to be their accountability partner and collaborate with them. Permission is key. Without it, you can be encouraging and leading, but too much and you'll come off as a control freak.

If someone does decide they want you to be a partner, collaborator, or mentor, the first thing is to focus in on their goals. The Art of Strategic Reaction (please visit kylebrost.com to learn more) speaks more on this front, but for the sake of this book, really get to know them. The more you can speak to their goals and desires, the better.

I am not a morning person, but I get out of bed 10X faster when I think about the great things that will come from a good day's work than just thinking about a day of work. Unfortunately, we all have tendencies to be short-sighted and undervalue our big goals. Being that reminder to others is step one.

After that, use the principles in this book. You have many of them. Help them set up action chains, make hard things easy to do, call out progress and make it visible, etc. There are enough tips, tricks, and processes in this book to help you give the best advice. They will look good, and you will feel the accomplishment of serving others. You might even be as good as Cordia Harrington, mentoring 17 people to achievement.

This effort of supporting others in their goals will not only help them, but it will also help you be more effective at escalating. Share this book, the process, and the tools with others, so they too can make progress and turn their potential into reality!

A FINAL WORD

You started this book by considering two choices. The first was to do nothing—with which you would gain nothing and lose nothing. The second was to take action, accepting that the chances of achieving your desired result were one in one hundred.

While it may seem like a silly scenario, it is a real one. It is a question you answer every day, sometimes dozens of times. Based on your actions, how have you been answering it?

If this book does nothing else, I hope it leads you to choose action more often. I sincerely hope it causes you to choose progress over fear, even just once.

The reality is that your chances of success aren't one in one hundred, they are virtually guaranteed if you just keep taking action. The results you expect may not happen, but success surely will.

Take action, be prepared for unexpected successes, value your potential, and cherish the growth you will experience.

You, my friend, will *Escalate* and so too will your achievements!

Escalate finds it's power in your potential and your goals. Considering this, it can only demonstrate it's power when your goals continue to grow. When goals are set and not worked on, they will become outdated.

The goals you set for yourself at 20 are different than those set at 30, 40, 50, etc. Do not let your goals become outdated! Aspire to more and *escalate*, you will discover potential within yourself that you have yet to imagine.

You, my friend, will *Escalate* and so too will your potential!

BIBLIOGRAPHY

1. Harden, B. (2015). *Escape from camp 14: One mans remarkable odyssey from North Korea to freedom in the West.* New York: Penguin Books.

2. Dyer, F. L. (2010). *Edison, His Life and Inventions.* Boston: MobileReference.com.

3. Garone, E. (2016, September 15). Capital—The man behind the million-dollar homepage. Retrieved September 8, 2018, from http://www.bbc.com/capital/story/20160914-the-man-behind-the-million-dollar-homepage

4. Summary, M. (2015). *The life-changing magic of tidying up: A detailed summary of Marie Kondos book -- The Japanese art of decluttering and organizing!!* Ten Speed Press; 1st edition (October 14, 2014)

5. McRaven, W.H. [The University of Texas at Austin]. (2014, May). *Admiral McRaven addresses the University of Texas at Austin Class of 2014.* Retrieved February 11, 2017.

6. Ambrose, S. E. (2013). *Undaunted Courage: Meriwether Lewis Thomas Jefferson and the Opening*. Riverside: Simon & Schuster.

7. History.com Staff. (2009). Lewis and Clark. Retrieved from https://www.history.com/topics/lewis-and-clark

8. Hechter, O., International Conference on Cell Membrane Structure. [Published 1972].

9. Kamenica, E., Ariely, D., & Prelec, D. (2005). Mans Search for Meaning: The Case of Legos. *PsycEXTRA Dataset.* doi:10.1037/e640112011-016

10. Amabile, T., & Kramer, S. (2011). *The progress principle: Using small wins to ignite joy, engagement, and creativity at work.* Boston, MA: Harvard Business Review Press.

11. McClelland, David C., John Atkinson, Russell Clarke, and Edgar Lowell. *The Achievement Motive,* by David C. McClelland [et Al.]. New York: Appleton-Century-Crofts, 1953. Print.

12. Dweck, C. S. (2017). *Mindset: Changing the way you think to fulfill your potential.* New York: Robinson.

13. Perry's greatest accomplishment has nothing to do with business. (n.d.). Retrieved August 3, 2018, from http://www.cnn.com/2009/SHOWBIZ/07/23/bia.tyler.perry/index.html

14. Finlay, B., & Finlay, C. (2017). *Kilimanjaro and beyond: A life-changing journey*. Nepean, Ontario: Keep On Climbing.

15. Kyle Korver vs. Perfection (2015, February). Retrieved September 12, 2018 from https://www.usatoday.com/story/sports/nba/hawks/2015/02/02/kyle-korver-vs-perfection-atlanta-three-point-shot/22693565/

16. Science of Railway Locomotion. (n.d.). Retrieved August 8, 2018, from http://www.brooklynrail.net/science_of_railway_locomotion.html

17. Sealed Air Corporation. (n.d.). Our History. *An Improbably Beginning*. Retrieved September 8, 2018, from https://sealedair.com/company/our-history

18. Lamborghini Cars Were A Result of a Tractor Company Owner Being Insulted by the Founder of Ferrari (2011, March). Retrieved on September 12, 2018. http://www.todayifoundout.com/index.php/2011/03/lamborghini-cars-were-a-result-of-a-tractor-company-owners-frustration-with-ferrari/

19. Wood, W., & Neal, D. T. (2007). A new look at habits and the habit-goal interface. *Psychological*

Review, 114(4), 843-863. http://dx.doi.org/10.1037/0033-295X.114.4.843

20. Graybiel, A.M. (1998). The Basal Ganglia and Chunking of Action Repertoires. Neurobiology of Learning and Memory, 70(1-2), 119-136. doi:10.1006/nlme.1998.3843

21. Hagura, Nobuhiro, et al. “Perceptual Decisions Are Biased by the Cost to Act.” *Elife*, vol. 6, 2017, doi:10.7554/elife.18422

22. Philadelphia approved a mandate to ensure a trash can is strategically placed outside any place that sells food to help reduce litter and stray trash (2015, December). EfficientGov Staff. Retrieved on September 12, 2018 from https://efficientgov.com/blog/2015/12/16/how-disneyland-influenced-philadelphia-waste-management/

23. Mark, G., Gudith, D., & Klocke, U. (2008). The cost of interrupted work. *Proceeding of the Twenty-sixth Annual CHI Conference on Human Factors in Computing Systems—CHI 08.* doi:10.1145/1357054.1357072

24. Deutschman, A. (2005, May). Change or Die. *Fast Company*. Retrieved from https://www.fastcompany.com/52717/change-or-die

25. Borgonovi, F. (2008). Doing well by doing good. The relationship between formal volunteering and self-reported health and happiness. *Social Science & Medicine*, 66(11), 2321-2334. https://doi-org.erl/10.1016/j.socscimed.2008.01.011

LEARN MORE

Use this code ESCALATE15893 to get 35% off the Escalate Course.

Visit: kylebrost.com/escalate

Access the most powerful resource to get yourself unstuck and achieve your biggest goal yet.

You'll get access to...

- **The comprehensive Escalate Assessment with a personalized jumpstart guide**
- **15+ Video modules**
- **Exclusive tools, templates, and guides to ensure your progress**
- **The complete outsourcing guide and checklist**
- **Weekly Live Q&A webinars and all recorded webinars**
- **FAQs and support from others just like you**

For free supplemental resources on Escalate, please visit:

https://kylebrost.com/escalate

ABOUT KYLE BROST

Kyle is a lifelong entrepreneur. He earned money to start his first company, a commercial carpet cleaning business, by working on the oil rigs in Wyoming. After running this company for three years, he sold it and started an international freight brokerage in Kansas City, Kansas. He ran this company for nearly four years before changes in the market forced his creative exit.

He has gone on to start or invest in companies in the fitness, family entertainment, consulting, education, and research industries.

Kyle is currently the CEO of Spark Policy Institute, where he leads an interdisciplinary team of consultants, researchers, and evaluators who make sense of messy social and environmental problems so that effective solutions can be implemented.

Through his company, Kyle Brost Intl, he offers consulting, training, and speaking on strategic thinking, strategic leadership, and organizational strategy. He has personally facilitated strategy development for over 100 organizations and has trained more than 1500 leaders on strategic thinking and leadership.

As an Inc. 5000 Entrepreneur, member of Forbes' Coaches Council, and Top 25 Influencer 2017, he speaks across the globe on improving strategy and "Doing Good, Even Better."

He is a regular Contributor to Forbes, The Good Men Project, Thrive Global, and Influencive.

When he isn't traveling, Kyle spends most of his time in Denver, Colorado, with his wife, three sons, Great Pyrenees dog, and tortoiseshell cat. He enjoys traveling, reading, listening to music, cyclocross riding, resistance training, and creating memories with loved ones.

Connect with Kyle

Website: kylebrost.com

Facebook: @brostkyle

Instagram: @kylebrost

LinkedIn: @brostkyle

Twitter: @kyle_brost

For Press, Speaking, or Consulting Inquiries Email

info@kylebrost.com

www.ingramcontent.com/pod-product-compliance
Lightning Source LLC
Chambersburg PA
CBHW031338040426
42443CB00006B/382

* 9 7 8 0 5 7 8 4 0 7 2 7 2 *